Creating Computer Programs for Learning

Creating Computer Programs for Learning: A Guide for Trainers, Parents and Teachers.

Gary W. Orwig, *Ed. D.*

Assistant Professor of Instructional Technology
University of Central Florida

Reston Publishing Company, Inc.
A Prentice-Hall Company
Reston, Virginia

Library of Congress Cataloging in Publication Data

Orwig, Gary W.,
    Creating computer programs for learning.

    Bibliography: p.
    Includes index.
    1. Computer-assisted instruction.   2. Programmed instruction.
3. Computer managed instruction.
I. Title.
LB1028.5.072   1983   370'.28'5   83-4597
ISBN 0-8359-1170-5
ISBN 0-8359-1168-3 (pbk.)

Apple II and Apple II E are registered trademarks of Apple Computer Company, Inc.

TRS-80, Models I and III are registered trademarks of the Radio Shack division of Tandy Corporation.

Commodore PET, CBM and Commodore 64 are registered trademarks of Commodore Business Machines, Inc.

© 1983 by Reston Publishing Company
A Prentice-Hall Company
Reston, Virginia 22090

10 9 8 7 6 5 4 3 2 1

Printed in the United States of America.
Interior designed by Dan McCauley

Table of Contents

Part 1

CAI Defined, 3

Non CAI Applications, 4

Clerical Aid, 4

Computer Managed Instruction (CMI), 4

Attributes, 5

Individualized, 5

Immediate Feedback, 6

Track Learner Progress, 6

Ease of Updating, 6

Limitations, 6

NOT a Human, 6

Highly Verbal, 7

Time-Consuming, 8

Drill and Practice, 9

Linear Tutorial Programs, 10

Branching Tutorial Programs, 10

Simulations, 11

The Real World of CAI, 12

Part 3

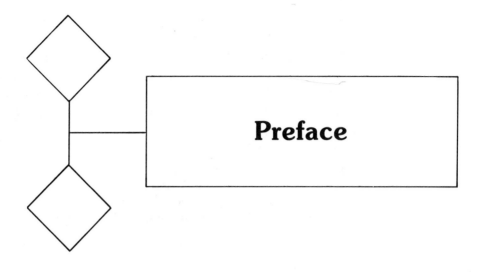

Preface

What Is This Book About?

Now that microcomputers are becoming commonplace in instructional settings, many educators are discovering that commercial programs frequently leave much to be desired. Partly due to this frustration over commercial software and partly due to the natural creative curiosity of educators, many are expressing a desire to "roll their own." This book shows how to use the BASIC language to create instructional programs for use on computers. It includes the elements of instructional design, charting out the instruction and translating the instruction into BASIC. Many examples of specific programming techniques are provided.

For Whom Is It Written?

This book has been written for all those who are interested in the important process of writing instructional programs for the computer. This includes teachers in the classroom, teachers enrolled in formal or in-service courses in computer-assisted instruction, college students studying instructional technology or related fields, industrial trainers, or parents (and kids) interested in using a home computer for more than video games.

What Equipment Is Needed?

When looking for a computer to use with this book, you could consider any of the following:

1.   Apple II or Apple II E computer with Applesoft BASIC
2.   Radio Shack TRS-80 Model I or III with Level II BASIC
3.   Commodore PET, CBM or Model 64 with Floating Point BASIC
4.   Any computer (micro or other) with floating point BASIC that allows undimensioned string variables and dimensioned string arrays

Other equipment is helpful.

Memory

The more memory that a computer has, the better. Because computer-assisted instruction tends to be a memory hog, 16k should probably be the minimum.

Disk Drive

This is not required, but it surely helps. A tape drive will be adequate to store and load your programs, but you will be limited in your ability to store student records automatically.

All material for this book has been produced on an Apple II computer. Because not all BASICs are equal, care has been taken to point out areas where differences occur. These differences are usually of minor importance to the instructional programmer.

What Do You Need to Know in Order to Use This Book?

To use this book, you need to have a beginner's understanding of BASIC. While this book does not use sophisticated applications of BASIC, it does not teach the initial steps of BASIC. You should know enough about your computer to get it running, to write a simple program, and to save that program. Usually the instruction manuals will get you that far. You also will need to know some things about the people for whom you are creating the instructional programs. Such things as reading skills, math skills, grade level, and personal interests are important. Finally, either you or somebody with whom you are working should be good with the subject matter. It can be embarrassing to write a technically good program that contains inaccurate information.

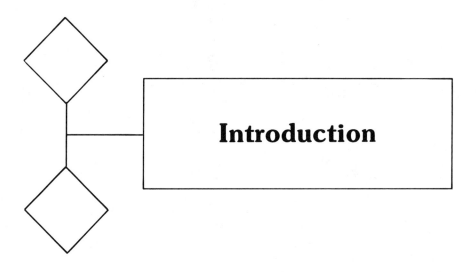

Introduction

Using a computer to teach certainly isn't a new idea. Those who were high school students in the early 1960s can remember the numerous magazine articles, motion pictures, and lectures that predicted an immenent computer explosion in the field of education. Computers did slowly enter the administrative areas of education (scheduling, record keeping, payroll, etc.), but they never seemed to become popular in the classroom. It was my senior year of college when I first saw a computer. By the late 1960s and early 1970s almost all public discussions of the computer as a "teacher" had ceased.

What had happened? Why did such a promising (or threatening) technology almost vanish? While a detailed examination of this question is beyond the scope of this book, one definite drawback of computers in the 1960s and 1970s stands out. They were appallingly expensive. One good-sized computer could easily equal the cost of a complete addition to a school (and those were the baby boom years). Almost all widely publicized computer-assisted instruction (CAI) projects of that era were funded through federal grants. Without federal money, no school system and certainly no educator could afford the use of a computer for instruction.

The times have changed. Sudden advances in technology have made the affordable desk-top computer a reality. Not only are the small, powerful computers found in many classrooms; they are also showing up in many homes. These new small computers (microcomputers) are impressive in their power.

Most current microcomputers are at least as powerful as some of the 1960s room-sized computers. In addition, they are intended to be used by only one person at a time. The infamous difficulties that time sharing created in some of the early instructional projects have become only memories. Since the microcomputer serves only one person, it can act almost instantaneously on any request that a person might give it. With the earlier constraints of cost and undependability eliminated by the microcomputer, it is no surprise that interest in computer-assisted instruction has once again exploded.

The computer revolution in instruction is taking place. Computers are quietly humming away in all kinds of instructional settings in public education, private education, industrial training, and private homes. As with many instructional innovations, the microcomputer has created somewhat of a fad. Many individuals seem far more concerned with the quantity and status of their machines and materials than with any true instructional values. Others are convinced that everything that can be taught can be taught better on a "micro." As with any other instructional medium, there are times when computer-assisted instruction should be used, and there are times when it shouldn't be used. Careful planning is needed to avoid the potential abuses of such a powerful instructional device. It is my intent through this book to establish the microcomputer as one more tool on the instructional workbench.

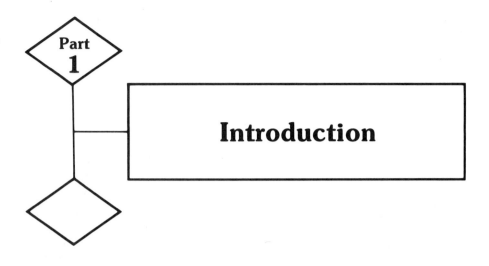

Introduction

This section introduces computer-assisted instruction (CAI) delivered through microcomputers. We examine the definition of CAI, when CAI should be used, the various types of CAI, and the types of equipment needed for successful delivery of CAI.

Quite a bit of computer terminology is introduced, so be prepared for frequent trips to the glossary. This working vocabulary is critical in communicating with others who are involved in CAI. In a short time you too will be able to speak computerese with the best.

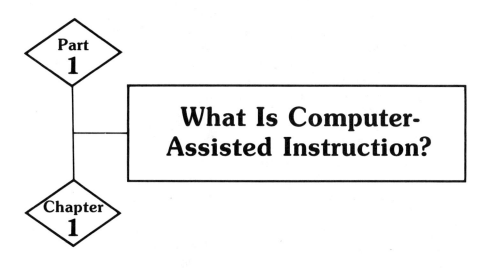

Part 1

What Is Computer-Assisted Instruction?

Chapter 1

CAI Defined

One of the first items on the agenda is to establish an operational definition of computer-assisted instruction (CAI). Throughout this text CAI is defined as an instruction which meets the following two criteria:

A.   The computer serves as the primary vehicle for the delivery of the instruction. What the computer actually delivers (the subject matter) can be almost anything. While many people associate CAI with math and science instruction, this is only because math and science teachers were among the first to experiment with CAI. Currently some of the most exciting CAI programs are in the areas of music education and creative writing.

B.   The learner and the computer are in direct communication with each other. This process is called "interaction," and it places CAI into a category of instruction shared with human instructors. While the computer at its best is a poor substitute for effective human interaction, it is far superior to most other nonhuman forms of instruction. A well-written CAI program is capable of proceeding at a pace determined by the learner. It is also capable of modifying the presentation of the instruction to match the capabilities of the individual learner. Contrast this with other forms of instruction (a video tape, or perhaps even a classroom lecture) which do not involve interaction and proceed at a fixed pace, with no consideration for the needs of individual learners.

In summary, an elementary student working through a vocabulary game on the computer would be involved in CAI. In a similar manner, an airline pilot is also involved in CAI when he or she is rehearsing landings at a new airport through the use of a computer simulation. The requirements of using the computer as the vehicle and having student-computer interaction are met in both cases.

Non-CAI Applications

Clerical Aid

Computers are also used in instructional settings under conditions that do not match the above definition of computer-assisted instruction. While these applications will not be covered in any great detail in this text, a couple of the more important ones need to be mentioned.

First, the computer can be used as a clerical aid. Given appropriate programs, it can be a word processor to help prepare tests, it can prepare worksheets, it can keep track of grades, and so on. Although the students will probably benefit from such applications, these applications cannot be considered as CAI since the students do not communicate with the computer on an individual basis.

In addition, clerical applications do not always involve the actual delivery of instruction (as in the case of grade keeping).

Computer-Managed Instruction (CMI)

An emerging application is the use of the computer to manage instruction. Given a sophisticated program, the computer could track the progress of each student through a variety of instructional activities. Depending on the needs and interests of an individual student, the computer might assign a chapter from a textbook, a motion picture, a laboratory experiment, or maybe even a lesson of CAI.

Computer-managed instruction (CMI) is currently being used in highly defined settings with some success, but even the best of the programs are quite limited in flexibility. The greatest problems arise in attempting to write a program which can accommodate the changing needs of the students and the changing instructional materials that might meet those needs. Presently this is one area where a qualified instructor still has a definite edge over the computer.

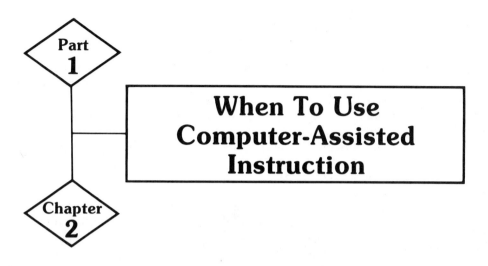

When To Use Computer-Assisted Instruction

Part 1

Chapter 2

Prior to getting into the mechanics of CAI, it is essential to establish the conditions that are most favorable for the use of computers in instruction. After any medium has been in use for a period, outstanding examples of its use and misuse surface. Through careful attention to those examples and the application of a little common sense, it is eventually possible to establish the best and the worst characteristics of that particular medium. While there are always some exceptions to any rules, it would be wise to try to use CAI in settings that maximize the attributes of the medium and to consider other alternatives in situations where the limitations prevail.

Attributes

Individualized

The microcomputer is designed for use by a single person at a time. Its keyboard can normally be used by only one person and usually operates on only one program at a time. As a result, the instruction provided works best if it is highly *individualized*. An individualized program is written to work with one person at a time and to consider that person's learning characteristics. To a bystander a well-written program may indeed look like several entirely different programs as different learners use it.

Immediate Feedback

The computer is capable of quickly evaluating learner input and acting on it. As a result, the learner can receive almost *immediate feedback* to the answers that he or she supplies to questions in the program. With the possible exception of testing situations, this immediate feedback has been shown to be highly motivating to learners. A well-written program can praise the learner for correct answers, correct him or her in the case of wrong answers, and even recommend an alternative learning strategy if the computer program is not doing the job.

Track Learner Progress

In addition to using student responses for providing immediate feedback, the computer can store the student's records (assuming that the proper storage devices are available). Thus, it is possible to use the computer to *keep track of learner progress*. Depending on how the program is written, these records can be used by the student as a review, by the instructor in keeping track of student progress, or by the computer to start the student automatically at the point where he or she left off.

Ease of Updating

Many topics being taught today change rapidly in content. Countries, states, and cities change names; inches change to centimeters; history changes as our viewpoint shifts. As these changes become apparent, it becomes necessary to change what is taught. Some forms of instructional materials, such as motion pictures, are virtually impossible to update locally. Others, such as mimeographed worksheets, beg for updating. CAI programs fall somewhere in between. It is usually a minor task for the author of a locally produced CAI program to change a name or date in it. On the other hand a commercially produced, "protected" CAI program can be as rigid as a motion picture. However, since this book is about locally produced instruction, for our purposes CAI is *easy to update*.

Limitations

NOT a Human

Computers, however, have several limitations, and these limitations must be kept in mind during the development of CAI.

Foremost, a microcomputer is *not* a human. It is no more sensible to rely on CAI to provide complete instruction than it is to rely only upon motion pictures or any other single medium. Even the best CAI programs cannot replicate all of the subtle attributes of a well-trained, ambitious instructor or parent.

For example, CAI probably does very little to encourage the development of the nebulous area of interpersonal communication skills, while an instructor can quite often draw an introverted individual into a group discussion. It is even possible that heavy doses of CAI might aggravate the condition of a seriously introverted individual. At the same time, a good CAI program, properly administered, can be a refreshing change of pace from the normal classroom or home study routine. Research indicates that CAI, when properly administered, is among the most effective of teaching tools.

Highly Verbal

There are situations where a picture is worth a thousand words, but in current CAI it may be easier to write the thousand words than to draw an acceptable picture. You may be dazzled by the high quality of graphics some commercial programs generate, but it is frustrating to discover that without the addition of expensive graphics tablets or light pens, there is no simple way to create a highly detailed picture on most microcomputers. It is fairly easy to create simple block-like (low resolution) pictures, but these have little use in most training situations. If not overused, such simple pictures can be used successfully to attract attention or to provide feedback.

What is an ambitious neophyte CAI programmer to do? You can either buy a lot of expensive peripheral equipment and spend a long time trying to learn how to use it, or you can start out by selecting instructional tasks which are *highly verbal* in nature. There are plenty of these tasks around, and there is certainly nothing wrong with creating instruction for them. About the only major consideration is that you *design the instruction so it is at a reading level appropriate for the learners*. As you become confident in the basics, you can gradually incorporate simple graphics for feedback and attention-getting. When high-quality graphics tools become reasonable you will be able to shift over to the production of graphically oriented instructional programs.

One final aspect of the problem with high quality graphics is high-quality motion. While simple animation of stick figures can be demonstrated on most microcomputers, such techniques have little application in training. Anything more complex is very demanding of even the most advanced computer programmers. As interested as you are in CAI, always try to keep in mind that there are still other instructional media in existence. For the time being, if motion is a necessary aspect of the instruction, forget CAI for that application. Consider instead a motion picture or video tape.

Time-Consuming

Finally, the task of producing CAI will be time-consuming. It is only sensible to create instruction for situations that will produce a *reasonable* payback. It may not be wise to spend 30 hours creating a 30-minute program that only one learner will use one time. On the other hand if 400 learners will use the program, the 30 hours will have been well spent.

In general the microcomputer is one more medium for instruction. What it can do well, it can do exceptionally well. However, some instructional situations are far more suited to other forms of media. As mentioned, a requirement of detailed motion would indicate the use of motion picture or video formats. A need for large-group instruction might indicate the use of more traditional approaches such as the classroom lecture. One must be objective. Don't consider the microcomputer a solution to every instructional problem. It is a promising medium that will work well in a fairly narrow range of applications.

Microcomputer CAI

Media Attributes and Constraints

Attributes

Individualized	Easy to update
Self-pacing	Simulations
Immediate feedback	Color
Track student progress	Graphics

Constraints

Highly verbal	Slow production
Not for large groups	Expensive to start
Extensive planning	Maintenance expense
Attention to detail	Author training needed

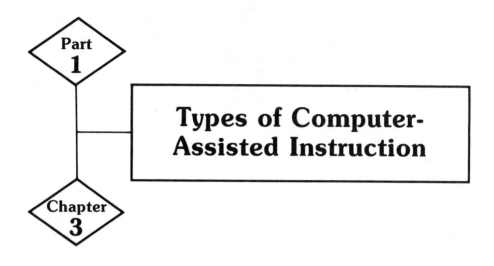

Types of Computer-Assisted Instruction

Computer-assisted instruction ranges from simple to complex in design. Over the last few years, levels of complexity have become fairly consistently labeled as follows:

1. Drill and practice
2. Linear tutorial programs
3. Branching tutorial programs
4. Simulations

These are not mutually exclusive categories. Programs within each category can vary considerably in complexity, and even the categories can overlap to some extent. There are, however, key conceptual differences among the categories that need to be explained.

Drill and Practice

Drill and practice is much the same no matter how it is done. Whether it utilizes pencil and paper or the computer, the intent is to reinforce an emerging concept through repetitive practice. Although frequently criticized as boring, time-consuming, and incapable of developing the "overall picture," drill and practice can be a useful instructional technique when used sparingly. Drill and practice has been found to be successful with basic math skills, vocabulary development, and areas that involve "paired associate" learning. In many situations existing devices may work at least as well as a computer program for drill-and-practice applications. Small handheld calculator devices work well for some math and language development areas for a fraction of the cost of a microcomputer. Needless to say, it is always wise to consider the available alternatives when faced with designing drill-and-practice instruction. On the other hand, it is a good technique with which the neophyte instructional program writer to start, since it is simple to design (see the sample drill-and-practice program in Appendix A).

Linear Tutorial Programs

Linear tutorial programs differ from drill and practice in that they are normally used as complete instructional tools. They can be used to introduce a topic, to refine the concepts involved in the topic, and to test attainment of those concepts. Probably the main descriptor of this instruction is *linear*. The instruction proceeds in a straight line or "chain," and every individual involved in the instruction follows precisely the same path through the instruction. While this single path makes linear instruction fairly easy to create, there is no way to allow for the individual differences of the learners. Fast or slow, informed or uninformed, every learner must proceed through every frame of the instruction.

In the design of such instruction, a major decision must be made. Should the instruction proceed at a slow pace, using small bites of material in each frame? Should the instruction proceed at a more lively pace, using large bites of information in each frame? In one case the designer risks losing the interest of the informed or fast learner, while in the other case the designer risks confusing the uninformed or slower learner. There is no simple answer to this dilemma. One solution lies in using this form of CAI mainly for groups that don't differ much in their individual learning ability or knowledge of the topic. Another solution lies in using linear programs primarily as testing tools to examine competency in concepts that have been developed through other instructional techniques. With a testing device, the instructor wants to ensure that every learner proceeds through measurement on every key concept or task in the instruction. The linear program is ideal for such an application (see the sample linear program in Appendix B).

Branching Tutorial Programs

The branching form of computer-assisted instruction brings the computer into the spotlight. Because of the flexibility of the computer it is possible to create branching instruction that is virtually unlimited in the number of paths for individual learners to take through the instruction. Previous attempts at branching instruction usually involved a special textbook. After a student answered a question in the book, he or she would turn the page to find what to do next. Depending on the answer, the student would be told to turn to one of several different pages. Some of these pages would contain various types of remediation (in the case of a wrong answer), while other pages would advance to other topics. The attempt to create such a book for any reasonably complex topic usually resulted in a nightmare, both for the instructional designer and the learners as they soon became totally "lost" in the book, forgetting which page they were going to as well as the page they came from.

This is where the computer can make a good idea work. The computer can serve as an invisible "page turner," showing the student only what he or she should see next. This process is called *transparency*, a technique of allowing a person to learn without letting the medium become a distraction. In a well-designed unit of branching instruction, the learner can be pretested so that only the unlearned material in the unit will be presented to the learner. As the instruction continues, the program can be written so that concepts are explained in greater detail only if the learner has trouble with the initial presentation. Finally, some programs have been written so that individual learning preferences (verbal descriptions versus graphic descriptions, etc.) can be accommodated.

In summary, while branching tutorial programs are more difficult to produce than linear tutorial programs or drill and practice, they have the potential to serve a much larger population of learners. Such programs will probably become the major form of computer-assisted instruction produced for commercial distribution (see the sample branching program in Appendix C).

Simulations

Imagine climbing into your two-seater single-engine plane and firing it up. After all the usual preflight checks, you taxi to the runway and open the throttle. Once up in the air and safely away from traffic, you try your hand at a few simple aerobatics and almost go into a dangerous spin. Having sufficient thrills for the day, you navigate your way to the airport, get into the landing pattern, and bring the plane down. Your landing was a bit bumpy, but no damage was done. At this point you take a deep breath, lean back in your desk chair, and turn off your computer. There was no airplane, just a computer model of one. This is a classic example of a computer simulation. With a properly designed simulation you are capable of gaining insight (and in some cases actual skills) in the operation of a system. Simulations may be of machines, ecological systems, or societal systems, to name only a few. In general a simulation becomes a sensible alternative when the real experience is too dangerous, too expensive, too slow, too rapid, or simply impossible to experience. In many cases a simulation can be used to build knowledge and skills (as in the case of the space shuttle) when it is impossible to practice on the real machine.

Unfortunately, even though good simulations can be fantastic training devices, they are difficult to produce. A major requirement is the ability to reduce the system that one is trying to simulate to a set of accurate mathematical formulas (*algorithms* in computer terminology). The computer uses these formulas to guide the progress of the simulation. Because the formulas can become complex, requiring many calculations every second, the microcomputer can become overtaxed. The end result is a simulation that is too slow, thus destroying much of its usefulness. This is frequently the case with "real time" simulations, like that of flying the airplane. To compensate for such limitations, some people have switched to using the native machine languages of microcomputers. While such languages can be processed much faster, they are complex and will not be covered in this text.

In summary, the simulation is potentially the most powerful teaching technique available on the microcomputer. It is also the most complex, requiring detailed subject knowledge and mathematic abilities. It is reasonable, however, to start with a fairly simple simulation that does not have to run in real time. A group car wash, a lemonade stand, a garage sale, or a patient-symptom-disease diagnosis process might be likely candidates (see the sample simulation program in Appendix D).

The Real World of CAI

Although there are four general levels of CAI, not all programs fit neatly into one of the levels. Instructional games, for example, can be drill and practice, branching tutorial, simulations, or a combination. The utilization of other instructional procedures such as problem solving or discovery techniques will also result in frequent overlaps.

There is nothing wrong with combining the levels. The most important factor is that the instruction work. The next most important factor is that you find the most efficient way to make it work.

Characteristics of the Four Levels of CAI

Drill and practice

Used to practice and refine an emerging concept
Repetitive, usually with increasing difficulty
Self-paced
Relatively easy to produce
Alternate forms of media might work just as well as computer

Linear tutorials

Usually used to teach an entire concept
Sequential, with every student following same path
Self-paced
Relatively easy to produce
Alternate forms of media might work just as well as computer

Branching tutorials

Usually used to teach an entire concept
Involves branching to accommodate variety of learners
Self-paced
Can be difficult to produce
Computer usually the superior medium for delivery

Simulations

Used to refine emerging concepts and skills
Individualized, but can involve teams of learners
Usually resembles some "real world" event
Can be self-paced but depends on what is simulated
Usually difficult to produce
Rarely anything superior to computer delivery

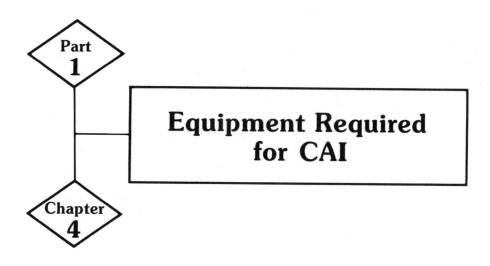

Equipment Required for CAI

Part 1

Chapter 4

Most average microcomputers are powerful enough to handle computer-assisted instruction without any problems. In fact, CAI is usually nondemanding of computers. During most of the time in CAI, the computer is patiently waiting while the learner is reading or otherwise reacting to material on the screen. However, several conditions will make life with CAI much easier for both instructors and learners.

The Viewing Screen

Because both learners and instructors will be spending many hours looking at the monitor, it should be the best that you can possibly afford. Too often a standard television receiver is substituted for an acceptable monitor. One of the worst selections in this category is the large-screen discount-store color television. While such a television may be satisfactory for watching Saturday morning cartoons, it will be full of distortion and fuzziness when used to present textual material.

The major problem with all standard televisions in computer applications is the fact that they are receivers. They are designed to pull television signals from the air and (through the channel tuner) convert the selected signal to a video signal to be presented on the screen. Most computers, on the other hand, are capable of producing pure video with no channel frequency attached to it. If the television (usually called a monitor) is designed to accept this video signal, it can completely bypass the tuner and all its associated distortion. Incidentally, much of the distortion in the tuner section of a television can come from the computer itself. Thus, a television that seems to work well for the Saturday morning cartoons may turn into a screen full of garbage when used with a computer.

Another problem with standard televisions is the size of the screen. For maximum viewing comfort the screen should be located directly behind and above the keyboard. The viewing angle (the angle that the eyes move through from one side of the screen to the other) should be no different than the viewing angle for ordinary reading material. The neck should not have to rotate to get the eyes from one side of the screen to the other. This means a preferred screen size of 9 to 12 inches, measured diagonally. Most standard televisions are too large.

Finally, there is the question of color. If a computer is capable of producing color images, should you use a color monitor or a monochrome (one-color) monitor? While color might be of value in certain forms of computer-assisted instruction (research has had a difficult time establishing the overall worth of color in training), there is a price to be paid. High-quality color monitors are extremely expensive. Because the face of a color picture tube is made up of small dots or lines of phosphors (the chemicals that create the colors), the process of controlling exactly what lights up and what does not becomes complex. The end result is that even with the best color monitors, fine detail (like letters in a word) will be somewhat fuzzy and color-fringed.

For less than the price of a poor color monitor, an outstanding monochrome monitor can be purchased. Monochrome monitors come with the standard black-and-white screen, but they can also be purchased with black-and-green or black-and-amber screens. The second and third use special phosphors to produce the green or amber colors. Some research indicates that both the green and amber screens cause less eye fatigue than the standard black-and-white screen.

The Computer

The best microcomputer to use for CAI is the one in front of you. While arguments will go on for quite some time regarding this topic, any microcomputer can be used for CAI. On the other hand, if you are shopping for a microcomputer to use specifically for CAI, there are some important characteristics to watch for. Selecting a computer specifically for CAI may make it less useful for some other area (such as word processing).

The Keyboard

The first item to examine is the keyboard. While in the store, you might only poke at one or two keys; when you get that computer into your home or classroom, you are going to have to live with the keyboard. The keys should be movable and standard size. They should also be in a standard arrangement. If you are unfamiliar with standard keyboards, compare the computer keyboard to that of an office typewriter. Pay special attention to the location of numbers and punctuation marks. If the keyboard has a separate number "pad," it should have the numbers along the top row of keys as well. It is irritating to reach over constantly to a separate pad each time a single number is to be typed. If at all possible, avoid flat calculator type keyboards. It is impossible to type with any speed on that kind of keyboard.

A brief diversion is in order at this point. Since natural language comprehension by even the largest of computers is far in the future, it will be a long time before we can talk to the microcomputers in any natural form. Single-word commands are possible if you have the right add-on equipment, but that is quite different from really talking to a computer. The end result is that we must deal with keyboards for quite some time. The more insistent we are about getting a standard form of keyboard, the more likely it will eventually appear on all microcomputers. With keyboard skills becoming so important, it is quite possible that typing will become as basic of a skill as math and reading.

Memory

Computer memory has become so inexpensive that it is no longer an issue, except with the smallest of microcomputers. Very simply, get as much as you can on the standard version of microcomputer that you are considering. Sixteen K (16 thousand characters) of program memory should be considered the absolute minimum for CAI. If you have less than that, your programs must be so short that they won't be able to teach much. Forty-eight K (standard on many micros) is a much more usable quantity of memory. The more memory the computer has, the larger the program it can work with.

Mass Storage

Since most microcomputers can work with only one program at a time, other programs must be stored in some manner. The two most popular storage mediums for microcomputers are the standard cassette tape and another magnetic device called the *floppy disk*. Computers can store programs on cassette tape by recording the information as a combination of tones. Later the tape can be replayed, and the computer will convert the tones into the commands of the program. This inexpensive process has been developed to the point where it works quite reliably for any one computer and tape recorder pair. Since each computer company uses a different process for creating and decoding tones, there is no compatibility of tapes from one brand of computer to another. It may be difficult to get a program from one computer to load into another computer of exactly the same type because individual tape recorders vary considerably in frequency response, volume, and speed characteristics.

Several other minor irritations exist when using cassette tape to store programs. Since it is possible to store a dozen or more programs on one standard tape, many people do so in order to decrease the number of tapes that they must keep on hand. Unfortunately, it is impossible to tell which program is which by listening to them. One set of beeps sounds like any other set of beeps. Thus, it is necessary to keep track of where each program begins and ends on the tape by watching the tape counter and keeping a written index. If a program in the middle of the tape is needed, the tape player is put into fast forward until the counter reaches the approximate location. Several tries are frequently required to find the exact start of the program. To complicate matters even more, some CAI programs store student progress so that an instructor can return and check to see what the students have done. To do this, the student must insert the correct tape (wound to the right position), press the record and play buttons of the recorder, then stop the tape and remove it when the computer is finished. Needless to say, many good programs have been accidentally recorded over by this process because the wrong tape was used or the correct tape was in the wrong position.

The Floppy Disk

The floppy disk, like cassette tape, stores program information on a magnetic surface. The disk, however, rotates; the computer controls the position of the magnetic head on the disk. The computer can also automatically start and stop the disk and keep track of what is stored on the surface of the disk. It is said to be a computer-controlled device, while the cassette tape is a user-controlled device. These features make the disk ideal for CAI applications. With long programs the computer can automatically fetch new chunks of the program as the learner works through those sections in the program memory. The computer can also automatically store the student's progress at the program end (assuming that the program is designed to do this—it is a complex process).

There are two distinct disadvantages of the floppy disk system, however. First, it is expensive. A single disk system can be 10 times more expensive than a single cassette tape system. Second, floppy disks are fragile devices. They are easily ruined by being touched at the wrong part, being bent, or being placed near sources of magnetism (like the picture tube area of a color television).

Which of the two systems you choose depends on economics and applications. In most cases, however, the floppy disk has the definite edge for CAI.

Upper/Lower Case and Other Details

Sooner or later you will discover that it is not fun to read a lot of lines of closely spaced, block upper-case letters. While this book provides examples in upper-case only for the sake of computer compatibility, serious CAI should have the option of displaying text in upper- and lower-case letters, where the lower-case letters have descenders (letters like p, y, and g, which go below the line). This is not a trivial task. While some computers are designed to provide upper- and lower-case, others simply can't or can do so only through the addition of expensive components.

Graphics

At times in CAI programs a graphic illustration is definitely needed. While most microcomputers have some form of graphics capability, there are absolutely no standards in the way that illustrations are created. Every computer company has its own way of creating graphics; some are clearly better than others. If graphics will be an important factor in your CAI, then make certain that you check the graphics capabilities of the computers being considered.

Sound

With the exception of music education, there are no major applications of sound in CAI. If it is available, it can serve as a cue device or a reinforcing device. Be careful to avoid overuse, however, because too much sound can become a real distraction.

Color

Should you buy a computer because it produces color images? As mentioned, research has failed to document a real need for color in training. There can be exceptions. If color cues are an essential part of the training task, then color is definitely needed. For example, a program designed to teach the process of reading the value codes of resistors in an electrical circuit would have to use color. This is because the codes are in color. Even in this situation there might be some problems, because the tint control on any color monitor might be adjusted improperly. If this were the case, the blue band on the resistor might actually show up as green on the screen. Needless to say, there are potential problems with the use of color in CAI.

In summary, there are some best choices if you have the luxury of selecting the microcomputer that you want to use for CAI. However, almost any microcomputer can be used if you are careful and don't exceed its limitations.

Desirable Characteristics of a Microcomputer Used for CAI

The screen

Video monitor (not receiver)—9 to 12 inches
Monochrome—green or orange image
Color—only if absolutely necessary

The keyboard

Standard size, movable keys
Keys in standard typewriter format

Memory

16 K of program memory the minimum
48 K of program memory sufficient for virtually all CAI

Mass storage

Disk system—almost essential for CAI
Cassette system—ok for limited applications

Upper/lower-case letters on screen

Very useful for text-oriented CAI
Lower case descenders on *p, y, j, q, g* preferred

Graphics

Low-resolution graphics almost essential
High-resolution graphics preferred for commercial programs

Sound/music

Essential only for specific applications, e.g., music education
Limited but general use as a cue

Color

Needed only for a few specific instructional applications
Requires expensive color monitor for acceptable detail
Might have some motivational values

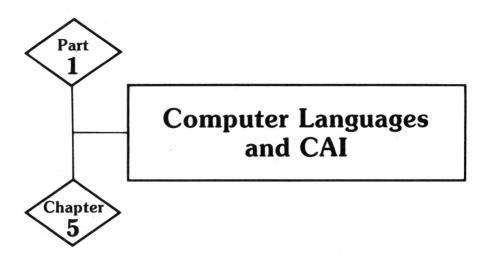

Part
1

Computer Languages and CAI

Chapter
5

The native language of computers consists of nothing but zeros and ones arranged in patterns meaningful only to computers. The language of humans frequently consists of many words and sentences with meanings that depend on how they are spoken. Such language is usually meaningful to only a select group of humans and never to computers. As a result of these differences, we cannot talk directly to computers and they cannot talk directly to us. Some form of translation device is required. The translation device is what we usually refer to as a high-level computer language. In truth, "high-level language" belongs no more to the computer than to us. It is instead a compromise. It is an agreed-upon syntax that both humans and computers follow. Although such a language is not efficient for either computers or humans, it does allow meaningful interchange of information.

There are actually four levels of computer languages, ranging from the native machine-code mentioned earlier to those languages that resemble the human language.

Machine Codes

Every computer has stored deep within it a primitive language based on codes of zeros and ones. Although these native languages differ from one brand of computer to another, each computer can converse and compute in its native language with blinding speed. Unfortunately, most humans simply can't cope with thousands of groups of zeros and ones. Within a short time all groups begin to look identical. The computer would still be a curiosity (and a dull one at that) if we could work only with machine codes.

Assembly Languages

The next step in the evolution of computer languages was to create a primitive translator called an *assembler*. The assembler allows a human to enter commands to the computer as short mnemonic codes, such as JMP for jump (no, that is not a physical command) or BRK for break (no, it doesn't involve physical violence). The assembler then translates these mnemonics into the zeros and ones of the computer's native language. Such a process makes life much easier for computer programmers because one mnemonic code can take the place of several groupings of the native code. Still, ordinary people will have trouble dealing with assembly languages. They are much too primitive for normal conversations.

Higher-Level Languages

Higher-level languages include virtually every language that goes beyond the mnemonics of the assembly languages. In most cases each can help the human and computer communicate on a wide variety of tasks, although any one might be specialized toward some particular area, such as word processing or statistical computations. All kinds of higher-level languages exist. Of those currently in heavy use, BASIC and Pascal are probably the most appropriate for the construction of computer-assisted instruction. You can instantly get into a heated argument in a group of computer addicts by stating that you prefer one or the other. The argument is about as productive as arguing over the superiority of English or French. They are simply two different languages, each with its own individual characteristics. Only because BASIC is most common on microcomputers have I chosen it for the examples in this book; I have nothing against Pascal.

Special Languages

Some high-level languages have been designed to do only one thing well. This concentration of effort allows the language to be sophisticated for that specialized task but practically worthless for others. We are most concerned about the specialized languages called "authoring" languages. These languages allow

CAI lessons to be typed into the computer with a minimum of trouble, but don't count on them to figure your income tax. PILOT is the only authoring language widely available for microcomputers. While some people claim that PILOT tends to mold instructors into working within a narrow range of all possible CAI activities, others feel that it is the most efficient way to generate large volumes of CAI quickly. If you plan to create much CAI, you should check to see if PILOT is available for your microcomputer, and if it is, you might try it. Because PILOT occurs in many "dialects," in most cases a PILOT program must be rewritten slightly when it is moved from one brand of computer to another. There are a few less widely known authoring languages, but consider using these only if you don't care about sharing (or selling) the products that you create.

Course-Writing Systems

It is possible to go one step further and create CAI through a course-writing system. The concept of a course-writing system is to allow a total novice at computers to enter an instructional program. The system leads the instructor through every phase of the authoring process. At every point instructions tell the person what to do next. Course-writing systems are usually complex programs (written in one of the high-level languages) in which the programmer has tried to anticipate every possible problem that the novice CAI writer could encounter. If the original programmer were thorough, the result is effective, although the CAI lessons are usually limited in diversity. On the other hand, if the original programmer failed to anticipate a major problem area, the novice CAI writer will end in a frustrating trap. In short, a "bug" in a course-writing system can make it worse than useless. These programs are new and usually work on only one type of computer. They show much promise, but for now use them at your own risk.

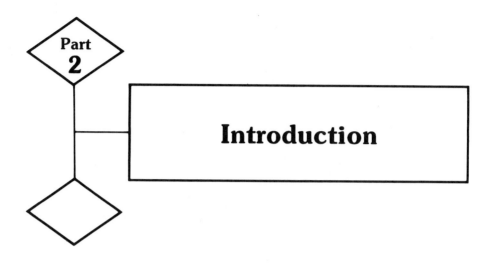

Part 2

Introduction

Now that you have a good idea of what computer-assisted instruction involves, you might be tempted to sit before your trusty computer and give it a try. However, CAI isn't an ordinary form of instruction. While an experienced instructor can constantly adjust content and style to meet the needs of the learners, a computer can't. The computer is fundamentally a fast, stupid machine. It can only do what your program tells it to do. For this reason you must anticipate all possible problems, explanations, and shortcuts that might be needed in the instruction and incorporate them into the program ahead of time. If you fail to do this, there will certainly be a time when a student takes an unexpected turn in the instruction and the program will not be able to tell the computer what to do. At this point the CAI will clearly have a "bug" in it, and you will have to attempt a repair (extermination?) job. It is never as easy to correct a flaw in a finished product as to design the product without the flaw.

Part 2 of this book provides an overview of instructional design, a relatively structured approach toward producing successful CAI programs. If you have had prior experience with instructional design techniques, this will be a good review. If you have no prior experience, this will be a good introduction. If you try it and like it, the bibliography provides sources of greater detail. If you try it and don't like it, I wish you luck. Indeed a few lucky souls can "intuitively" produce excellent CAI with no visible signs of preplanning. However, the only way I can produce good CAI is to spend hours of time with careful instructional development before I begin writing the program.

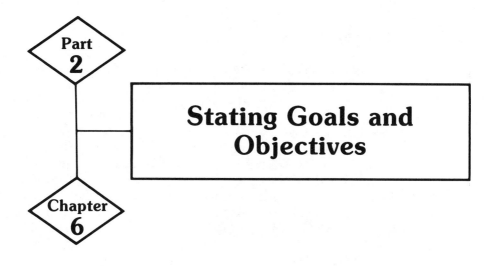

Part
2

**Stating Goals and
Objectives**

Chapter
6

Goals

One of the most difficult aspects of instructional design is the process of getting started. Before you attempt to write a CAI program, you must carefully think about what you want it to do. If you don't clearly state the goals, you will quickly lose track of what it is you are trying to teach. It is important at this stage to separate your personal goals as an instructor from the instructional goals of the students. While your goal may be to teach metric measurement with the least amount of fuss, this may not be consistent with the instructional goal set for the students.

A goal can usually be stated by answering the following question: What should the learner get from this program? An example of an instructional goal might be: Upon completion of this program, the student will understand synonyms and antonyms. A good instructional goal concentrates on the ultimate effect that the instruction should have on the learner. In the eyes of the learner it should be practical and attainable. The following example would be less desirable as an instructional goal: Upon completion of this program, the learner will be able to write five pairs of synonyms and five pairs of antonyms. It is premature, at the stage of writing goals for instruction, to get caught up in the process of measuring the instruction. There will be plenty of time for that in the next step. It is possible to have more than one goal for a unit of CAI if the goals are closely related. If you discover that you have several widely divergent goals, you will probably need more than one CAI unit.

Objectives

People involved in public education often recoil into self-defensive postures when they hear the term *behavioral objective* tossed into a conversation. Teachers have been abused by behavioral objectives many times—and behavioral objectives have been abused by teachers as well. If improperly used, they can direct instruction into narrow paths, forcing the instructor to ignore any inquiries that might deviate only slightly from those paths. The end result, some educators say, is the stifling of creativity and the encouragement of teaching for a specific test. Others claim that the use of objectives is forcing many educators to face the fact that they don't know what they are trying to teach. They claim that the process of writing objectives will establish the use of more efficient teaching techniques and will eliminate much wasted time in education today.

What is the fuss all about? For those who don't know what a learning objective is, it is quite simple in concept. (Notice that I have used the terms *objective*, *behavioral objective*, and *learning objective*. We will consider them all to be the same.) Briefly, a learning objective has the following characteristics:

1.   A description of the behavior expected of the learner as a result of the instruction

2.   A description of the conditions under which the learner is expected to demonstrate the behavior

3.   A description of the minimum acceptable level of performance

Description of Desired Behavior

It is virtually impossible to judge whether a student has learned something unless you can observe a change in the student's behavior. The change might be reciting a poem from memory, solving an algebraic equation, or designing a new integrated circuit. It is easy to describe behavior that is psychomotor in nature (skills requiring eye-hand or other mind-muscle control). It is also relatively easy to describe the desired behavior if it is cognitive in nature (involving recognition, recall, concept formation, problem solving, or synthesis).

On the other hand it is most difficult to describe desired behavior in the affective domain. How would you describe behaviors that would accurately indicate a change in attitudes, values, or beliefs? Part of the problem is the inherent deceptiveness of the human spirit. For example, after lengthy instruction designed to convince people that the world will end on October 1, 1999, how do you determine if you were successful? Can you give people a test? Can you ask them? Can you secretly observe them? How can you determine that you changed their attitudes? There is no simple answer. The process of writing behavioral objectives is weak in the affective domain.

Since this book deals primarily with getting started in CAI, I recommend that we bypass lengthy philosophical arguments and proceed. We will stick with the psychomotor and cognitive areas. The behavior component of an objective should contain an action verb of some type. Examples of such verbs are *construct, repair, recite, recall, classify, describe, solve, create, predict,* etc. Thus, a behavior component of an objective might be something like: Students will identify antonym pairs.

Conditions

The conditions of an objective establish all the restrictions (and aids) that influence the demonstration of accomplishment of the objective. For example, students working in teams of 4 and using a standard dictionary will identify pairs of antonyms from a supplied list of 20 words.

Standards of Acceptable Performance

The objective should clearly state what is required to demonstrate competency. This may be stated in terms of percentage correct, maximum time required for completion, maximum allowable deviation, or whatever measure is appropriate for the objective. An example of a complete objective would be this: students working in teams of 4 and using a standard dictionary will identify all pairs of antonyms in a supplied list of 20 words. In this case the simple word *all* establishes the minimum acceptable level of performance. It could just as easily be 80 percent or 90 percent within a 10-minute time span. A number of factors determine the performance level required of any particular group of students on any particular objective. Whenever possible the standards should reflect performance as it would be required in the real world.

Enabling Objectives and Terminal Objectives

The major objective describing the key topic that you wish to teach is called a *terminal objective*. The main characteristic of a terminal objective is that its accomplishment usually indicates the end of a lesson or portion of a lesson. In reaching that major objective, however, smaller objectives must be met. These smaller objectives are called *enabling objectives*. Careful definition of a terminal objective, along with its required enabling objectives, results in an outline for a unit of instruction.

Sample Learning Objectives

1. Conditions

Given the type and thickness of 5 flat pieces of metal

Expected behavior

Select appropriate drill bit, speed, and pressure for each

Criteria

100 percent accuracy

2. Conditions

Given 10 two-minute excerpts of classical music

Expected behavior

Identify the full name of each composer

Criteria

A minimum of 8 of the 10 correct

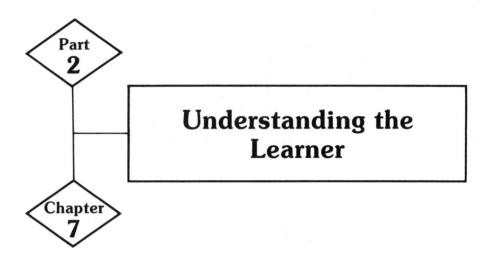

Part
2

Chapter
7

Understanding the Learner

Instructional designers frequently tend to assume too much about the learners with whom they are dealing. As a result, much of the instruction that they have written has failed, or at best has had to be revised greatly. It is best to understand clearly the assets and limitations of the people with whom you are working before you try to instruct them. The process of collecting and studying this information is frequently called *learner analysis*.

Tool Skills

While there are several important factors to consider, by far the most important are those skills required at the beginning of the instruction. These required "tool" skills must match the entry skills of the learner in order for the instruction to be successful. It is senseless to create CAI heavily oriented toward reading if your learners can't read. While the tool skills that are required vary from project to project, there are some obvious ones to check. First, reading is most important. You should know the average reading ability of your learners, and you should write at a vocabulary level that does not exceed this. Depending on the program and its emphasis on reading, you might even design it to adjust to the reading level of individuals. Math abilities are frequently second on the list of tool skills. Much of what we do in CAI tends to be math-oriented.

You should establish measures of the basic skills of your learners in this area if it is relevant. Typing might even be a necessary tool skill if the training will involve a lot of keyboard entries.

Beyond language, math, and typing, the list tends to become diverse. One good technique for establishing required tool skills is to look carefully at those learning objectives that you have identified as enabling objectives. For any enabling objective there are "enabling" enabling objectives. In other words for every skill to be learned, there are preliminary skills that must be known. Since you can't teach absolutely everything in one lesson, you must draw a line. At the point where you draw the line, every preliminary skill becomes a required tool skill; you must acknowledge that a learner will have problems with the lesson if he or she lacks those tool skills.

At times the entry skills of a learner are limited by physical or maturational factors. For example, young children may not have the ability to use the keyboard accurately. Programs written for children should make minimal use of the keyboard and should be "forgiving" when incorrect keys are accidentally struck. Children learning to read may have trouble with the block upper-case letters presented on the screen by some computers. While there isn't much computer flexibility in this area, it is sometimes possible to use the computer's graphic abilities to draw large upper- and lower-case letters on the screen. Adults are not immune to such problems. Bifocal glasses and computer monitors simply don't mix. For adults with "aging" vision, try to keep the monitor as close to the keyboard as possible in order to avoid the "stiff neck" syndrome from bending the head back too far. For learners with physical disabilities, you might have to modify your computer to provide suitable access. For example, there are large keyboards that can be used by learners who are partially paralyzed.

Other Factors

Some important characteristics of learners are created by societal factors. A program written for students in San Diego might not work with students in New York City. Even though skill levels might be similar, you might find the two groups don't speak the same language. While pronounced regional differences in dialect seem to be fading somewhat (possibly due to national television), there are still some major differences in how Americans communicate with each other. When working with recent immigrants, it is quite possible that instruction will be more efficient when provided in their native language.

Finally, some characteristics of learners are hard to categorize. For example, you would probably discover that a group of art majors might study and learn a foreign language using methods that are different from those followed by a group of math majors. Within each group you would undoubtedly find individual preferences as well. Research is beginning to indicate that some people tend to be verbally oriented, while others seem to be nonverbally oriented. Some individuals prefer highly structured instruction, while others prefer to develop their own structure as they proceed. As this point it is too early to make any accurate determinations of individual learning styles, but it is an area of research that is worth watching.

The process of conducting a learner analysis can be a formal affair for a group of "unknown" students, complete with the administration of standardized examinations. On the other hand it can be an informal process for a group of familiar students. In this case the instructor usually puts onto paper (in some organized manner) the characteristics that he or she already knows about the students. In either case the learner analysis should serve as a major guiding device in CAI design.

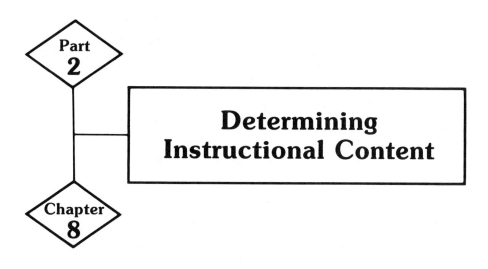

Determining Instructional Content

The actual content of a CAI program is best determined by a process called *task description*. In the task description each terminal objective is carefully analyzed in order to determine all enabling objectives. In the process notes are kept regarding any particular order or priority that must be followed to make the instruction successful. The individual steps (tasks) are then recorded in some orderly fashion.

Sample Task Description

Add Two 3-Digit Numbers

Preparation

    Locate paper
    Locate pencil
    Copy first number onto paper
    Copy second number onto paper
        Make certain columns are aligned
        Make certain numbers are vertically spaced properly
    Draw line under second number

Addition

    Add the two digits on the right side

(continued)

Sample Task Description (*Continued*)

Addition (*cont.*)

Write the sum below the line in right column
    If sum is 2-digit, place right digit below line and place left digit above top center number (carry)
Add the center column
    Include carry digit if there is one
    If sum is 2-digit, place the right digit below line and place left digit above top left number (carry)
Add the left column
    Include carry digit if there is one
    If sum is 2-digit, place the right digit below line and place the left digit to the left of it

Finished

Learning processes may be either active or cognitive in nature. For example, the process of learning to change an automobile tire is active, while the process of learning to select antonym pairs is cognitive. While it is possible to conduct a task description of each type, most people find it much easier to start with an active task.

There are two types of active tasks. An active task can require the same sequence, no matter who does it, or it might be possible to achieve the same terminal goal through a variety of routes. The first type is usually referred to as a *linear* active task, while the second type is usually referred to as a *variable sequence* action task. Linear tasks are especially easy to describe because there is little confusion over what comes next. One popular technique for preparing a task description of a linear active task is to "flow chart" it. While flow charting can also be used with variable sequence and cognitive tasks with some success, it falls right into place with the linear active tasks. Flow charting is a technique of utilizing a set of standardized symbols to depict graphically the individual components of some process (see Figure 8-1). The process of flow charting is one of individual preference. Some people find that the construction of flow charts is the only way to understand the individual steps in instruction, while others detest the limiting nature of the process. The only way to determine your own attitudes is to try it a few times (see Figure 8-2).

Begin, end

Process

Decision

Input, output

Connector

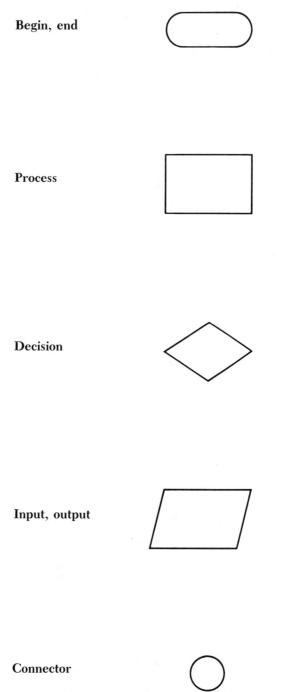

Figure 8-1. Some Common Flow-chart Symbols

Topic: Adding two two-digit numbers

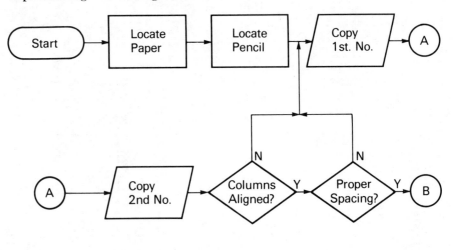

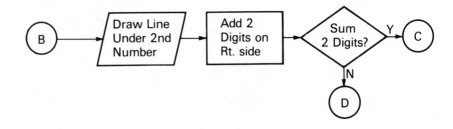

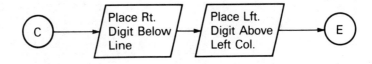

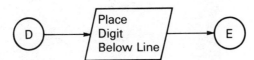

Figure 8-2. Sample Flow-Chart

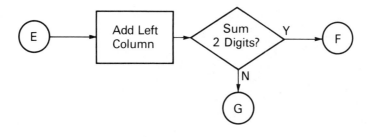

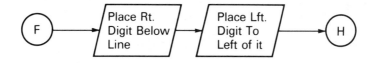

Figure 8-2. (*Continued*)

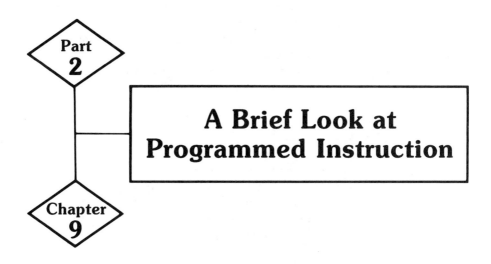

A Brief Look at Programmed Instruction

A great deal of what is to be learned about CAI can be learned by studying the texts that deal with programmed instruction (PI). While PI hasn't been at the front line of education lately, it is an instructional technique that has been researched and documented to a far greater extent than most forms of instruction. Many of the most successful techniques of PI are the most successful techniques of computer-assisted instruction. Many people argue that until CAI becomes more sophisticated, it is simply PI delivered over the medium of the computer. Whatever the outcome of the argument, there is a great deal of overlap of techniques and terminology. Since we can't turn this into a text on programmed instruction, we review only a few of the main concepts. Any person who is considering serious CAI writing should by all means dig out one or two of the PI texts listed in the bibliography and plan for a couple evenings of careful study. The amount of useful information gained will more than cover the expenditure of time.

The Frame

The frame is a single page of the instructional program. For CAI, the frame is one "screen" of the program. Frames can serve a variety of functions.

Introductory Frames

Introductory frames appear at the beginning of the instruction and at the beginning of each new concept within the instruction. They provide a preview of what is to be learned. Such frames are sometimes called *advanced organizers* because they get the student thinking along the right path. In CAI, introductory frames can also be used to collect from the student information such as name and age. Such information can be used later in the instruction to personalize the program.

Pretesting Frames

Pretesting frames serve two distinct purposes. They ensure that the student has the necessary entry skills for the instruction, and determine if the student knows any of the forthcoming instruction. If the student lacks the required entry skills, he or she should be given options for corrective measures whenever possible. If the student already knows some of the material, the program should be written so that the student automatically bypasses that part of the instruction.

Teaching and Testing Frames

Usually the heart of the instruction consists of one or more teaching frames followed by a testing frame. Depending on the design of the instruction, the results of testing frames may cause the program to "branch" to "remediation" frames, which are simply teaching frames designed to clarify a concept. There are a number of options in the design of teaching-testing frames.

Practice Frames

At times it is desirable to reinforce emerging concepts with practice. Practice frames most frequently occur just before major criterion tests. Generally the frames proceed toward more and more highly refined examples of the concept.

Criterion-Testing Frames

At the end of the instruction, a criterion test determines whether the accomplishment of all enabling objectives has lead the way to the accomplishment of the terminal objective of the unit. If the CAI is linear and a wide variety of students are using it, a number of students will need additional work. On the other hand, if the program branches effectively and the group is fairly homogeneous, it is quite possible that few will need additional training on the topic.

Teaching and Testing Frames—A Closer Look

RULEG–EGRULE

When you are trying to teach a new concept to students, it is better to provide the definition (or rule) of the concept, followed by examples, or to provide the examples, refining them until the definition is obvious? This question has been asked so many times that it has developed its own mnemonic aids. If the rule is taught first, followed by examples, the technique is referred to as the RULEG (rule before example) technique. If examples are provided first, followed by the rule, the technique is referred to as the EGRULE (examples followed by rule) technique. In general it is better to use the EGRULE technique when the students first encounter new material. On the other hand if students are working in an area where they already have a good deal of background, the RULEG technique might be more efficient.

Types of Responses

The responses of students can be covert or overt. Covert responses require no external actions. If you ask the student to think of the answer to a question but you don't require that it in some way be recorded, you have required a covert response. Covert responses have a definite problem. There is no way to tell if it is the correct response or if there is any response at all. Covert responses are used very little in CAI. Overt responses, on the other hand, require some action on the part of the student. Since the overt response must be entered into the computer, the program can evaluate it and take appropriate action. The following discussion deals with several types of overt responses.

Constructed-Response Frames

The constructed-response frame is best described as a fill-in-the-blank sentence. In this type of frame the student must "construct" the answer. There is no multiple-choice or true-false condition, where additional cues are apparent. The only major concern in the design of such a frame is that the blank occur somewhere between the middle and end of the key sentence. It is not desirable to put the blank at the beginning of the sentence. Such front-end loading creates confusion, causing the student to reread the sentence many times. While the constructed-response frame may be simple to design, care must be taken to provide the learner with all needed information in the proper sequence. In using CAI, this information must be narrowly defined, or there will be so many variations in the answers that a sophisticated program will be required to weed out the unacceptable answers from the the acceptable answers.

Selected Response Frames

There is a wide variety of frames possible where the student selects the answer from some set of choices. The most common of these are:

True-false
Multiple choice
Matching
Discrimination sets

Both true-false and multiple-choice frames are extremely easy to create for CAI. If you can write good, unambiguous true-false questions, you can program them into CAI. If you can create a typical multiple-choice question, you can put it into a CAI frame. All of the usual precautions still apply, but no special measures are required. If you are not experienced with objective question writing, it is best that you check a test and measurement book. Such information is too detailed for this book.

Matching questions are popular in programmed instruction, but there are complications when they are used in CAI. The major problem deals with screen control. It is hard to put two lists on the screen and then move down along the blanks next to one of the lists as the matching proceeds. It is even harder to write the program so that students can make changes in earlier selections, as they often do in matching problems. This process is not impossible, but it might not be the first place for a greenhorn to start.

Discrimination sets are a bit like matching. A concept is stated, then a list of candidates for the concept is given. The student is then asked to discriminate between the items in the list and select those that are appropriate for the concept. Such frames are fairly easy to create if each item in the list is presented sequentially.

Prompting

When a student first starts a new topic, he or she may need a good deal of guidance in arriving at the correct responses. Such assistance, when built into the program, is called *prompting*. Some people feel that prompting should be designed so that a typical student need never make an incorrect response. Such prompting would be heavy at the beginning of the lesson and would taper off as the student's familiarity with the content grows. Prompting can consist of many forms.

Set Frame

The set frame is a constructed-response frame in which the answer is simply a rephrasing of a sentence already in the frame. If the student reads carefully, he or she will be able to fill in the blank based on information on the screen.

Occasionally an even greater cue is created by underlining the correct answer in the text; this is about the maximum level of prompting normally used. It is most appropriate at the beginning of a new lesson.

Discrimination-Frame Distractors

The typical multiple-choice or matching question can be easy or hard, depending on the choices. The "wrong" answers are called *distractors*; the closer they resemble the "right" answer, the harder the question will be. A common form of prompting is to start with distractors that are greatly different from the desired response and then to "fade" these differences away as the concept is developed.

Hints

There may be times when a person simply doesn't know what to answer. Rather than risk frustration, it is wise to build into the program the option for providing hints. This option may require the pressing of a special key, or it may be automatic, based on elapsed time while waiting for an answer. In either event the hint should be designed to give the student a good chance of getting the correct answer; otherwise it is a waste of time. The use of a hint should also be recorded by the CAI program as a need for further work on that aspect of the lesson.

Feedback

As a student progresses through instruction, it is necessary to provide him or her with information regarding progress. In today's jargon these progress reports are called *feedback*. Depending on the circumstances, feedback can be either immediate or delayed, detailed or brief. Besides simply providing the student with a clear understanding of how he or she is doing, feedback can also be motivational in nature. In many CAI programs an animated figure congratulates the student on chosing the correct answer. Students enjoy the little creatures and try hard to get correct answers so that they can see them. Needless to say, feedback regarding incorrect answers should be carefully planned. It is not a good idea to be humiliating or punishing in the responses for incorrect answers; at the same time you must not inadvertently create a reward for the wrong answers. There are few classic examples of mistakes in CAI as yet (it is too new), but one is certain to be the vocabulary program that sank a battleship for each incorrect answer. Students became far more interested in sinking the ship than in learning the desired vocabulary; some students carefully prompted other students on which wrong answers most rapidly sank the ship.

Most of the time feedback should immediately follow the answer to a question. If the question is answered correctly, the feedback should be positive, personalized, and motivating. If possible, positive feedback should vary so that the student doesn't get tired of the same "Good going, Joyce!" given for every correct answer. It is also a good idea to repeat the correct answer as reinforcement. A response such as "I agree with you. Ten centimeters is the correct answer, Joyce." is such an example. In the case of an incorrect answer, there should be little fanfare. Probably it is best simply to tell the student that he or she is incorrect and then send the student back to try again. In the case of a branching program, the student can be sent down a path of remediation before the concept is retested. In any event the program should be written so that a student is not permanantly trapped in a try-again loop if he or she can't answer the question. At this point the computer would actually interfere with learning; this would quickly build frustration. Similar potential problems are discussed under the topic of transparency.

Delayed Feedback

There are times when you may not want to give a student immediate feedback. At the end of a unit of instruction you may give a series of questions over all the major concepts in the unit. In such a situation it might be best to wait until all of the questions are finished before you provide details of the results. This would tend to minimize unnecessary emotional tension on the part of the student during the test. At the end of the test you would provide a summary of the student's performance on all the questions.

Step Size

It is probably appropriate to close this section on programmed instruction with a discussion of the most difficult aspect of PI for the inexperienced instructional writer. The quantity and level of information that you place in each frame determine the step size of the instruction. If you take small steps, the instruction will seem slow and dull. If you take large steps, concepts will be developed so quickly that many students will become confused and frustrated. There is no simple cure for inappropriate step size. If they are too small, you can't simply eliminate some of them. You will have to rewrite them into larger chunks. If the steps are too large, you might be able to add remediation branches of smaller steps where they are needed, but this is no small task when it comes to changing the CAI program.

While determination of proper step size comes with experience, several procedures will help minimize potential problems. First, the learner analysis is critical. Make certain that you know the key characteristics of your learners.

What do they know about the topic? What are their general academic backgrounds? How well can they read? Have they used PI or CAI? Second, remember that you probably know a lot more about the topic than they do. As you write the instruction, keep in mind that you will use it to train students, not yourself. Do not assume that they will understand a minor concept just because you do. Finally, make certain that you try your lesson on others as you are developing it. Assuming that you write it on paper before putting it into the computer, you can have typical students (and subject experts) check it out "in the rough." The earlier any modifications are made, the easier they are to make. The rough trial technique is discussed in the next section when we go into the process of storyboarding.

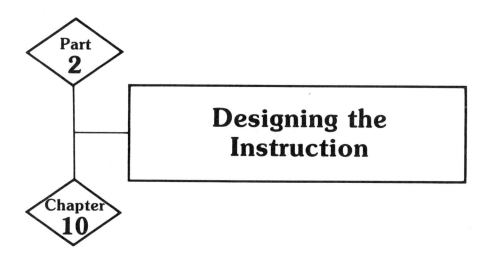

Designing the Instruction

It is now time to begin creating the actual instruction. Probably the most successful technique for this process is called the *storyboard*. A storyboard is created by writing individual frames of instruction onto 4- by 6-inch cards, then setting the cards on a bulletin board or table. The resulting storyboard allows you to visualize the actual content and flow of the instruction before you begin committing it to a programming language. More important, you can have some interested bystanders view the instruction and offer suggestions for modification. Try not to let your ego be completely shattered at this point. A route of instruction that seems perfectly logical to you might not be so to other subject experts. At any rate, if changes are needed, it is much easier to make them at this stage than later, when you are putting together the computer program. For programs that involve extensive branching, it is usually easier to work with storyboards of smaller parts, each of which represents an individual branch.

The specific content and arrangement of each storyboard frame will vary, depending on individual preferences. The closer each frame can represent each individual screen of the computer program, the easier it will be to assess the logic of the instruction. The following sample frame (Figure 10-1) includes many of the most important details.

Front of card

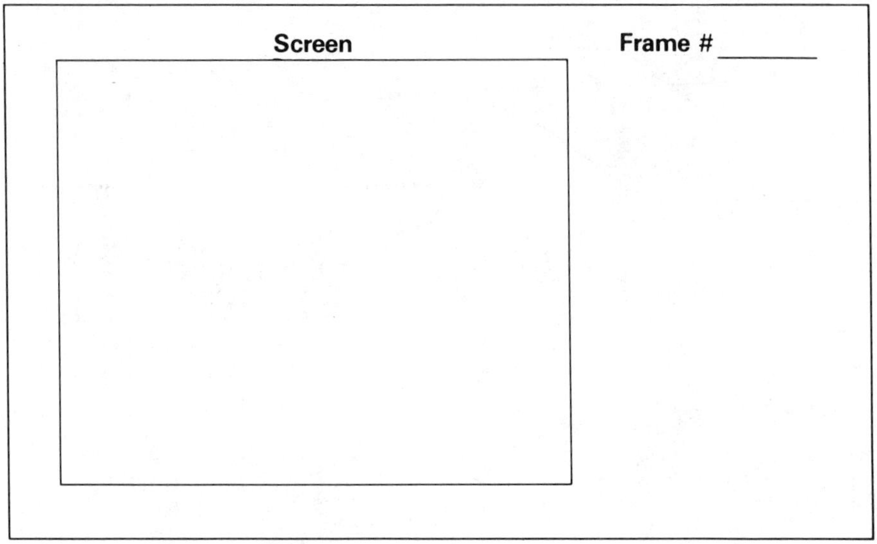

| Screen | Frame # _____ |

On card:

Screen

Frame # _____

Back of card

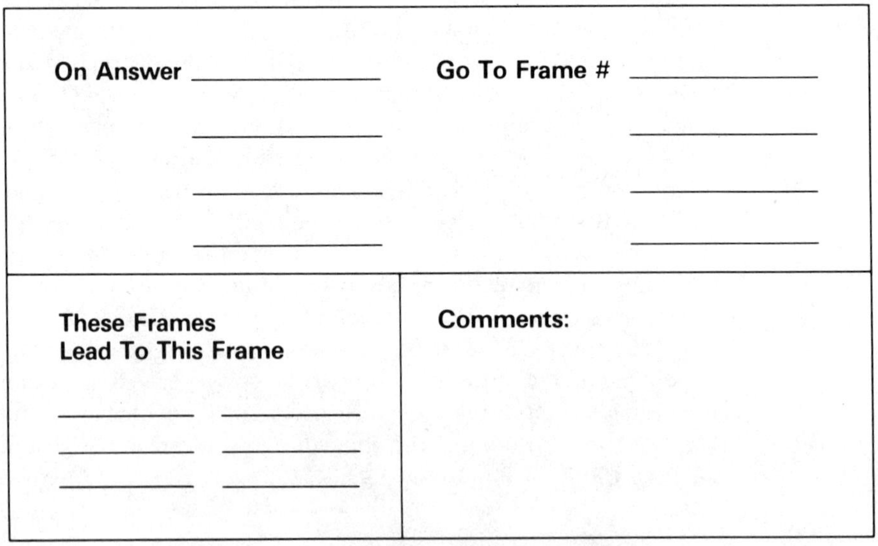

On Answer _____   **Go To Frame #** _____

_____   _____

_____   _____

_____   _____

These Frames
Lead To This Frame

_____ _____

_____ _____

_____ _____

Comments:

Figure 10-1. Sample Storyboard Frame Card

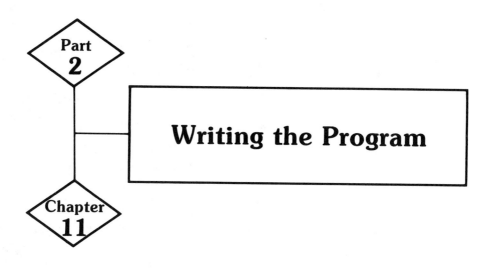

Part
2

Writing the Program

Chapter
11

Once your storyboard has been tested and revised as necessary, it is time to translate the instruction into a computer program. Since the BASIC language is a widely used and fairly consistent language among microcomputer brands, it was chosen for the examples in this book. However, life will be much easier in dealing with BASIC if you can locate several "utility" programs for your specific computer. While not all of these programs are always available for all the common microcomputers, they are becoming popular. Check with a dealer to find out which ones you can get.

Utility Programs

A *renumber* utility allows you to rearrange the numbering of a program (or section of a program) to suit your needs. If one of the routines in this book is exactly what you need but isn't numbered properly, a utility program is the answer. You can type in the routine exactly as it is in the book, then use renumber to change the numbering automatically to meet the needs of your program. A good renumbering utility will go through the entire program, changing all references to any section of the program that you renumber.

A utility that can *merge* separate program segments allows great flexibility in the way that you write programs. If you find a great subroutine in one program and want to use it in another, you can isolate the subroutine, renumber it to suit your needs, and then merge it into your new program. With this technique it is possible to store large numbers of subroutines on tape or disk and then use merge to assemble your programs from them. If you don't enjoy typing things over and over, this is a great way to prevent it.

One problem with collecting subroutines from a variety of sources is that they invariably use variables (pun intended) that you don't want to use. While it is possible to go through carefully and replace each old variable manually with the name you want to use, there is definitely an easier way. By using a good *variable replace* utility, you can load the program segment in which you want to make changes, state the variables that you want to change, give the new names, and then let your computer automatically edit in the changes. In the wink of an eye you have a subroutine that meshes perfectly with the rest of your program.

Sometimes things go wrong in a program. Lines don't work; variables interact with each other; everything is a general mess. Eventually you may get the program to work, but by then you have lost track of what is where in the program. A *document variables* utility will go through your program and show you every variable that you have used and on which lines you used each. Quite often you will discover that you aren't using some variables at all, or you are using some in places where you hadn't intended to use them.

Program Guidelines

Transparency

When a device is used to deliver instruction, the less it gets in the way, the better the instruction will be. For example, an old motion picture projector that takes 15 minutes to thread, produces jumpy pictures, and has terrible sound can be quite a bother. By the time the film is finished, most students will know more about the projector than about the film. The same problem can occur with computer-assisted instruction. If the computer becomes a distraction, the content of the instruction will suffer. The term *user transparency* is appropriate here. If the instruction is to be effective, the device that delivers the instruction needs to be as *transparent* to the user as possible.

Probably the major distraction in CAI is the computer *crash*. The *crash* is defined as an unexpected interruption in the delivery of the instructional program. An entire book could be written about the origins and cures of the thousands of types of computer crashes, but only a few obvious ones will be covered here. There are basically two types of crashes. Some crashes originate in the computer equipment itself, while the vast majority originate in the programs written for the computers.

Hardware Crashes

The major cause of equipment (hardware) crashes is the presence of either too much or too little electricity. Unless you are willing to buy an expensive battery backup system, you can't do much about too little electricity. A power drop that is sufficient to make the lights blink will almost certainly confuse a microcomputer. Try to ensure that your computer is not plugged into the same circuit as any piece of equipment with a big motor (such as a refrigerator, an air conditioner, a water pump, or a building elevator). If your whole house has many power drops, complain to the power company. It might be that too many houses have been added to a single transformer.

Too much electricity, on the other hand, can be managed. The major source of too much electricity is simple, and seemingly harmless, static electricity. That tiny little spark that you see and feel during cool, dry weather is a computer killer. The obvious solution is to eliminate the spark. You can raise the humidity in the area, spray your carpet with a commercial static shield—which you can buy in most office supply stores—or place an antistatic mat on the floor in front of the computer. Too much electricity can also enter through the power line. Power-line surge protectors are quite effective and relatively inexpensive. They will not protect the computer against a direct hit from lightning, however. Unless you have a great insurance policy, the best advice is to turn the computer off when the thunder is loud enough to scare the dog.

Software Crashes

A software crash is simply a defective program. When you write CAI, make certain that you try every possible route that it can take before turning it over to students. Quite often an obvious typographical error will be lurking in one of the seldom-used branches.

If the program is free of typos and logical errors, the next major problem area is the keyboard input process. If the correct answer to a question is *12*, what happens when the student types in *twelve*? Some microcomputers will simply come to a crashing stop, while others will respond with a highly informative message, like *redo from start*. In either case the instructional value rapidly begins to fade along with the computer's transparency. A carefully written program either will tell the student exactly what format to use or will accept a wide variety of equivalent answers.

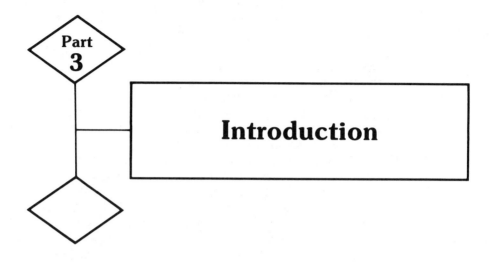

Part
3

Introduction

The third part of this book provides sample routines that can be applied to computer-assisted instruction. It is important for any program writer to develop his or her personal set of routines because their consistent use will save a great deal of time and will make the inner workings of the programs much easier to understand later. While there may be a tendency for a new program writer to overuse the same set of routines, an opposite effect usually occurs. Since the writer isn't busy trying to do the same basic things a different way each time that they are encountered, he or she has more productive time to spend with new and innovative approaches to the more challenging aspects of each new program.

Before you plunge into the world of CAI through BASIC, several points need to be emphasized. First, I must assume that you have had at least a brief introduction to BASIC programming. If you understand the uses of number and string (word) variables, PRINT statements, IF-THEN's, FOR-NEXT's, and the screen control processes (clear the screen, cursor movement, etc.), you are ready to tackle this material. If all this sounds like a foreign language, you had better do a little hands-on homework before going further. While computer manuals themselves are rarely of any direct value to beginners, a number of excellent introductory BASIC books are available. Classes are offered in most communities through computer stores, computer clubs, or public education.

Second, you should be aware that these routines were written on an Apple II computer with floating point (Applesoft) BASIC. Some of the routines will not work as expected on other computers unless changes are made. The following section provides details on different BASIC dialects and locations where changes are likely to be needed.

Finally, many of the routines are written so that they reside in a sample program. Frequently this sample program consists of a short main program followed by several *subroutines.* The sample programs have been written this way for the sake of clarity and ease in extracting those portions of each program that might interest you. However, in real life a portion of a program isn't usually placed into a subroutine unless it needs to be accessed from several other locations in the program. The "slow print from data" program shows two listings, each doing the same thing. The first listing places all the routines into subroutines, while the second listing places the routines consecutively in the main program. Which is better? It doesn't matter for CAI. As long as you have enough memory in your computer, any way that works is good. You should try to keep things organized, however. You may have to return to a program to make changes in a year or two, and you will regret it if you don't have good REM statements and a clear program flow.

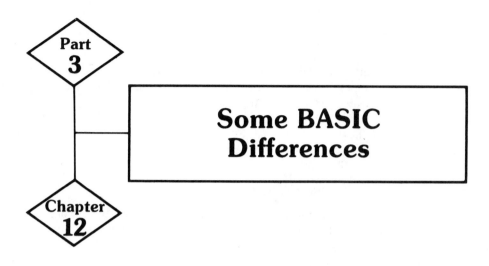

There are a few differences in the BASIC languages used by some of the favorite computers. While these differences are usually minor and just a bit annoying, they can sometimes have surprising effects on a computer program. Following are the most common differences a person would encounter in writing CAI programs on Apple II, Radio Shack Model 3, and Commodore CBM computers. These computers make up the majority of computers used in instructional settings. The following discussion assumes that you have at least a beginning knowledge of BASIC for your computer. If you haven't and you get lost, dig into your manuals and supplementary books to catch up. Try examples with your own variations until you are satisfied that you understand. As you work through the routines in this part of the book, keep in mind that they were written on an Apple II. They will sometimes need to be modified to fit your computer's BASIC dialect.

Clearing the Screen

Apple II	100 HOME
Radio Shack	100 CLS
Commodore	100 PRINT "see note"

Note: For the Commodore, the clear key is pushed between the quote marks in the PRINT statement. The result is a strange graphic symbol shaped like a heart. Commodore users quickly grow accustomed to this and other graphic symbols that represent screen controls.

Tabs

Both horizontal and vertical tabs are frequently used to move the cursor to a new position for printing. Generally tabs allow the cursor to move over previously printed material without erasing it.

Apple II

```
100 VTAB 12
110 HTAB 16
120 PRINT "HELLO"
```

No matter where the cursor is to start with, this set of tabs will position it 12 lines down from the top and 16 spaces in from the left margin. The word "HELLO" will then be printed at that location. On the Apple, the tabs are *absolute*, meaning they are always referenced to the upper left-hand corner of the screen.

Radio Shack

```
100 PRINT @ 540, "HELLO"
```

The preceding line will place the word "HELLO" in approximately the middle of the screen by using the PRINT @ command (usually called *print at*). Each line has 64 spaces, and you have to add up the spaces to get to the desired position.

Commodore

```
100 PRINT "(press the HOME key)"
110 PRINT "(press the CRSR down key 12 times)"
120 PRINT "(press the CRSR right key 18 times)"
130 PRINT "HELLO"
```

On the Commodores the cursor control keys can be placed directly into PRINT statements. The results are strange-looking graphic symbols, but they work well. The result of the preceding program is as follows. The HOME command returns the cursor to the upper left-hand corner without erasing anything. The next two lines move the cursor down and then across the screen. The final line prints the word *HELLO* approximately in the middle of a 40-column screen. By returning to the upper left-corner (HOME) for every tab, you can establish absolute referencing. This means that the same tab sequence will always produce the same results, no matter where the cursor started.

Randomizing

The process of creating random numbers in a program uses the same function but in different ways on different computers. In all cases, the expression between the parentheses in RND(esp) can be either a number or a variable.

Apple II

    100 A = RND (1)

This line will assign a randomly selected value to the variable A each time the line is encountered in the program. The value for A will always be a decimal between 0 and 1.0.

    100 A = RND(0)

This line will assign to A the same value that was created by the RND function the last time it was used. This is not of much use for normal CAI applications. If the expression in the parentheses is a variable, then it can be set to 0 to prevent creating a new value for A.

    100 A = RND(−1)

When a negative number is used in the RND command, a set value will be returned. A different value will be assigned to A for each negative number used. On top of this, RND will behave differently after a negative number has been used. After a negative number, RND(1) will always follow a set sequence of values.

Radio Shack

    100 A = RND(15)

The variable A will have an integer value between 1 and 15. The number in parentheses acts as the upper limit and can be any number or variable having a value up to about 32,000. This is the easiest form to use if you want a random integer.

    100 A = RND(1)

This one doesn't do much on the Radio Shack computers. It does work according to the preceding description. You continually get the value 1 back.

    100 A = RND(0)

This will return a random decimal between 0 and 1. This is the same as RND (1) on the Apple II.

    100 A = RND(−1)

It appears as though any negative number in the RND statement produces an error on my Radio Shack.

Commodore

100 A = RND(15)

The use of positive numbers greater than 1 is not specified in the Commodore manuals, but it appears to work the same as the following RND (1).

100 A = RND(1)

The use of RND(1) will produce a set sequence of "random" decimal numbers between 0 and 1.0. Depending on the individual computer, this same sequence may repeat every time that the computer is started.

100 A = RND (0)

This will produce random decimal numbers based on factors within the internal clock of each Commodore computer. When executed repetitively from within a program, this function will produce a different sequence every time that it is run. Because it is based on the system clock, strange results can occur when the RND(0) function is a part of a tight loop. The most common indication of this problem is "random" numbers that appear to be surprisingly consistent.

100 A = RND(−2)

A separate series of "random" decimal numbers is supposed to be produced for every negative number used in the parentheses. If a variable is used in the parentheses, and its negative value is created by another random function, then you can approach a "true" random number generator.

Note: While Commodore produces excellent computers, the firm is known for constantly making changes. The manuals don't always keep up with those changes. You may have to experiment a bit to get the exact random function that you want on your Commodore.

Keyboard Checking

The following routines check to see if a key has been pressed on the keyboard. This is useful for "press any key to continue" or similar subroutines. The exact details for these routines should be checked out in your specific computer manual. They can be a bit confusing.

Apple II

100 GET A$

When the computer reaches this line, it will stop and wait until a key is pressed. When a key is pressed, the value of the key will be stored in A$ (or any other variable) and the computer will proceed to the next line. It is best to use a string variable, because a letter key typed into a number variable will cause an error.

```
100 IF PEEK (49152) < 128 THEN 100
100 A$ = CHR$ (PEEK (49152))
120 POKE (49168, 0)
```

As written, these lines will seem to have the same effect as the GET statement for Apple II. However, this is a dynamic keyboard check routine. In line 100, you could follow the THEN with some line number other than 100. In that case, the computer would check to see if a key had been pressed; if not, it would go on to something else. There is a method to this apparent madness. The function PEEK looks directly into a location in the computer's memory. If this location is less than 128 in value, a key has not been pressed. If it is greater than 127, then a key has been pressed and the memory value is the ASCII code value for that key. The POKE function issues a command directly to a memory address, which then resets the keyboard for the next key press. While PEEKS and POKES are a bit clumsy, this is the only way to have an Apple check the keyboard without forcing it to wait for a key to be pressed. Such a routine is often used to time how long it takes to press any given key.

Radio Shack

```
100 A$ = INKEY$
110 IF A$ <> "Y" THEN 100
```

This two-line routine forces the Radio Shack to wait for the "Y" key to be pressed. This is a dynamic process like the Apple PEEK and POKE routine. In this case the computer actually jumps back and forth between lines 100 and 110 until the proper key is pressed. If you use the following line as the second line, the computer will simply sit and wait until *any* key is pressed.

```
110 IF A$ = "" THEN 100
```

Note that there is nothing between the two quotation marks. This is actually the *null* character and it simply means that there is no value for A$ when it was tested.

Commodore

```
100 GET A$
110 IF A$ = "Y" THEN 200
120 IF A$ = "N" THEN 300
130 GOTO 100
```

The action of the GET in the Commodore is virtually identical to the action of the INKEY$ with Radio Shack and the PEEK–POKE routine of the Apple II. In this example the computer will accept either a "Y" or an "N" and act accordingly. This assumes that you write something at lines 200 and 300 for the computer to do. Once again, if no key is pressed, the computer will hover in the 100-130 loop indefinitely.

Miscellaneous

Graphics

There are so many differences in graphics that there is no hope of covering three different brands of computers in this chapter. If you are interested in graphics (and you should be), go to your local bookstore or computer store and look through the books that deal with graphics on your specific model of computer. There most likely will be several, and you should be able to find one to your liking. Don't let the total lack of uniformity in graphics discourage you. Even though there are as many graphic approaches as there are models of computers, almost all are logical and straightforward (unless you want to paint a work of art). In a short time you should be able to construct simple graphic enhancements for your programs.

STR$ Function

While the STR$() function is not frequently used in CAI, it can be helpful during the manipulation of numbers. A$ = STR$(X) will convert the numeric value of X into a string for A$. This can be used to manipulate numbers with all of the string manipulation functions like LEN, LEFT$, MID$, and RIGHT$. It appears as though the Radio Shack and some Commodore computers automatically insert a space in front of the number during the conversion to a string. This can be a problem if you don't realize that it is there. It can be removed by stating A$ = RIGHT$(A$,X), where X is one less than the total length of the original A$.

PRINT Statements

The Radio Shack computer allows powerful PRINT @ and PRINT USING commands that can greatly simplify complicated printing routines. These commands are so popular that it is likely that you will find "enhancements" for other computers that will allow them to use similar commands.

   When using PRINT statements, you must consider the width of the computer screen. Programs that have been designed for a 40-character per line screen will look like they have been squashed to the left side of a computer screen that is capable of showing 80 characters per line. The converse situation usually produces pure nonsense on the screen. Eighty characters do not fit well on smaller screens. It may be necessary to reformat PRINT statements to make the best use of the computer screen in front of you.

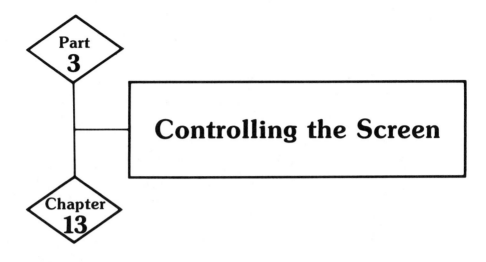

Part
3

Controlling the Screen

Chapter
13

While many program writers know what they want to put in the individual frames of their instruction, they have a great deal of trouble controlling the manner in which the information actually appears on the screen. The following routines are intended to help you present material in an orderly fashion.

Scrolling Routine

While global screen-clearing commands (such as HOME for the Apple or CLS for the Radio Shack) are effective in wiping out the entire screen, there are disadvantages to their use. They are instantaneous and remove everything on the screen. They also leave the cursor at the top of the screen. While this is fine in most cases, it forces you to place everything at the top of the screen.

The following simple scrolling routine allows you to use repetitive blank PRINT statements to control the amount and location of information on the screen. If used after a screen-clearing command, it has the effect of a vertical tab. If used repetitively without screen clearing, information appears to flow onto the screen from the bottom and off the screen at the top. In either case it is a pleasant change of pace.

```
*******************************
*                             *
*      SCROLLING ROUTINE      *
*                             *
*             ORWIG           *
*******************************
```

```
10   REM  A SCROLLING ROUTINE WHICH USES PRINT STATEMENTS
100  REM   START MAIN PROGRAM
110  REM   L SETS THE NUMBER OF LINES TO SCROLL
120 L = 12
130  REM  GO SCROLL
140  GOSUB 1010
150  PRINT "THIS IS A SAMPLE OF SCREEN SCROLLING."
160  PRINT "IN SOME WAYS IT IS BETTER TO USE"
170  PRINT "THAN COMPLETELY CLEARING"
180  PRINT "THE SCREEN."
190  PRINT
200  PRINT "IT SEEMS TO MOVE THE INFORMATION"
210  PRINT "UP THE SCREEN."
220 L = 9
230  GOSUB 1010
240  REM   END MAIN PROGRAM
250  END
1000  REM   START OF SUBROUTINE
1010  REM   SCROLLING ROUTINE
1020  FOR I = 1 TO L
1030  PRINT
1040  NEXT I
1050  RETURN
```

```
*******************************
*                             *
*      SCROLLING ROUTINE      *
*                             *
*    -->TABLE OF VARIABLES<-- *
*                             *
*******************************
```

```
I - COUNTER
1020 1040

L - LINES OF SCROLLING
120 220 1020

END OF VAR. LIST
```

Timed-Pause Scrolling

Adding a delay counter to the scrolling routine allows you to incorporate automatic delays in the presentation of material. This works fine for the display of short messages (such as positive feedback), but don't try it with long messages.

Because of the major, individual differences in reading speed, you will not be able to establish an appropriate delay time for long messages. Some students will be finished with the message (and probably wondering why nothing is happening), while other students will be only partly finished when the delay finishes and the program continues.

```
*******************************
*                             *
*     TIMED-PAUSE SCROLLING   *
*                             *
*           ORWIG             *
*******************************
```

```
10   REM    SCROLLING WITH TIMED PAUSES
100  REM    START OF MAIN PROGRAM
110  REM    L SETS THE NUMBER OF LINES TO SCROLL
120 L = 12
130  REM    GO SCROLL
140    GOSUB 1010
150    PRINT "THIS IS A SAMPLE OF SCROLLING"
160    PRINT "WITH TIMED PAUSES."
170 L = 14
180  REM    GO SCROLL
190    GOSUB 1010
200  REM    DE SETS THE LENGTH OF TIME TO DELAY
210  REM    THE LARGER DE IS, THE LONGER THE DELAY
220 DE = 1500
230  REM    GO DELAY
240    GOSUB 2000
250    PRINT "AS YOU CAN SEE, THE PACE IS "
260    PRINT "AUTOMATICALLY SET BY THE VALUE OF 'DE'"
270    PRINT "IT IS BEST TO USE TIMED PAUSES FOR"
280    PRINT "VERY SHORT MESSAGES."
290 L = 12
300  REM    GO SCROLL
310    GOSUB 1010
320 DE = 3500
330  REM    GO DELAY
340    GOSUB 2000
350 L = 24
360  REM    GO SCROLL
370    GOSUB 1010
380  REM    END OF MAIN PROGRAM
390    END
1000 REM    START OF SUBROUTINES
1010 REM    SCROLLING
1020   FOR I = 1 TO L
1030   PRINT
1040   NEXT I
1050   RETURN
2000 REM    DELAY COUNTER
2010   FOR I = 1 TO DE
2020   NEXT I
2030   RETURN
```

```
******************************
*                            *
*    TIMED-PAUSE SCROLLING   *
*                            *
*   -->TABLE OF VARIABLES<-- *
*                            *
******************************
```

```
DE - DELAY VALUE
220 320 2010

I - COUNTER
1020 1040 2010 2020

L - LINES OF SCROLLING
120 170 290 350 1020

END OF VAR. LIST
```

Flashing-Key Prompt

When you present a lot of information on the screen, it is best to let each student determine when he or she is ready to continue. This can be accomplished by placing an obvious message at the bottom of the screen, which tells the student what to do. The most common technique is to tell the student to press any key to continue. The following short routine works only on the Apple II because of the unique FLASH and NORMAL commands. It places the flashing message at the bottom of the screen. If you were to use this routine on other computers (without the flashing), you might also have to modify the VTAB and GET statements, as explained in the previous section.

```
10   REM   THIS IS A ROUTINE FOR APPLE
20   REM   TO PAUSE UNTIL ANY KEY IS PRESSED
30   REM   THIS ROUTINE USES COMMANDS UNIQUE TO THE APPLE
40   REM   THEY ARE FLASH AND NORMAL
100  REM   START MAIN PROGRAM
110  GOSUB 1000
120  REM   END OF MAIN PROGRAM
130  END
```

(continued)

```
1000   REM   START SUBROUTINE
1005   REM   WAIT FOR KEY PRESS
1010   VTAB 23
1020   FLASH
1030   PRINT "PRESS ANY KEY TO CONTINUE";
1040   NORMAL
1045   REM   STORE PRESSED KEY IN A$
1050   GET A$
1060   HOME
1070   RETURN
```

```
     *****************************
     *                           *
     *    FLASHING-KEY PROMPT     *
     *                           *
     *    -->TABLE OF VARIABLES<--  *
     *                           *
     *****************************
```

```
A$ - KEY PRESSED
1050

END OF VAR. LIST
```

Scrolling-Key Prompt

The scrolling-key prompt routine will place a horizontally scrolling message at the bottom of the screen. While not a true horizontal scroll (as in a theater marquee sign), the message will be attention-getting. This routine checks to see if any key has been pressed. If one has, the computer is instructed to return to the main program. As long as you adjust the program with the appropriate substitutes for lines 1020, 1030, and 2020, it should work on any microcomputer.

```
     *****************************
     *                           *
     *    SCROLLING-KEY PROMPT    *
     *                           *
     *            ORWIG           *
     *****************************
```

```
10   REM   THIS IS A SCROLLING PROMPT KEYBOARD
20   REM   CHECKING ROUTINE FOR APPLE
100  REM   THIS AREA WOULD BE THE MAIN PROGRAM
110  GOSUB 1010
120  HOME : PRINT "FINISHED"
130  REM   END OF MAIN PROGRAM
```

(continued)

```
140   END
1000   REM   START OF ROUTINES
1010   REM   CHECK KEYBOARD
1020   IF   PEEK (49152) <  = 128 THEN 1050
1030   POKE 49168,0
1040   RETURN
1050   REM   ASSIGN MESSAGE TO A$
1060 A$ = "PRESS ANY KEY TO CONTINUE"
1070   GOSUB 2000
1080 A$ = "                          "
1090   GOSUB 2000
1100   GOTO 1010
2000   REM   PRINT ROUTINE
2010 AL =  LEN (A$)
2020   VTAB 23
2030   FOR I = 1 TO AL
2040   PRINT  MID$ (A$,I,1);
2050   FOR J = 1 TO 20: NEXT J
2060   NEXT I
2070   PRINT
2080   RETURN
```

```
*******************************
*                             *
*     SCROLLING-KEY PROMPT     *
*                             *
*    -->TABLE OF VARIABLES<--  *
*                             *
*******************************
```

```
A$ - MESSAGE TO SCROLL
1060 1080 2010 2040

AL - LENGTH OF MESSAGE
2010 2030

I - COUNTER
2030 2040 2060

J - COUNTER
2050 2050

END OF VAR. LIST
```

Paused-Scrolling-Key Prompt

The only problem with the earlier routine is that the prompt begins the instant the routine is accessed. This action at the bottom of the screen can be a distraction to people trying to read information elsewhere on the screen. It seems almost as if the computer is impatient to start. A good "press any key" prompt should attract attention only when it becomes obvious that it is needed. The following routine will place the "press any key" message at the bottom of the screen, where it will sit passively for a preset period of time. After this period, it will begin to scroll as in the preceding example. At all times, scrolling or not, the computer is "watching" the keyboard for its signal to go on. If the delay in line 1040 is set to the appropriate value, the message should start to scroll only when it becomes obvious that the student is taking much too long and probably doesn't know what to do next. Once again you may have to modify the parts of the routine that deal with checking the keyboard and vertical tabbing.

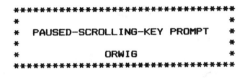

```
************************************
*                                  *
*   PAUSED-SCROLLING-KEY PROMPT    *
*                                  *
*              ORWIG               *
************************************
```

```
10   REM   THIS IS A PROGRAM WITH A GOOD KEYBOARD
20   REM   CHECKING ROUTINE FOR APPLE
100   REM   START OF MAIN PROGRAM
110   REM   THIS AREA WOULD BE THE MAIN PROGRAM
120   GOSUB 1010
130   HOME : PRINT "FINISHED"
140   REM   END OF MAIN PROGRAM
150   END
1000   REM   START OF ROUTINES
1010   REM   CHECK WITH NO SCROLLING
1020   VTAB 23
1030   PRINT "PRESS ANY KEY TO CONTINUE"
1040   FOR I = 1 TO 250
1050   IF   PEEK (49152) <   = 128 THEN 1080
1060   POKE 49168,0
1070   RETURN
1080   NEXT I
2000   REM   CHECK WITH SCROLLING
2010   IF   PEEK (49152) <   = 128 THEN 2040
2020   POKE 49168,0
2030   RETURN
2040   REM   ASSIGN MESSAGE TO A$
2050 A$ = "PRESS ANY KEY TO CONTINUE"
2060   GOSUB 3000
2070 A$ = "                              "
2080   GOSUB 3000
2090   GOTO 2000
3000   REM   SCROLLING ROUTINE
3010 AL =   LEN (A$)
3020   VTAB 23
3030   FOR I = 1 TO AL
3040   PRINT   MID$ (A$,I,1);
3050   FOR J = 1 TO 20: NEXT J
3060   NEXT I
3070   PRINT
3080   RETURN
```

```
*******************************
*                             *
*PAUSED-SCROLLING-KEY PROMPT  *
*                             *
*   -->TABLE OF VARIABLES<--  *
*                             *
*******************************
```

```
A$ - MESSAGE TO SCROLL
2050 2070 3010 3040

AL - LENGTH OF MESSAGE
3010 3030

I - COUNTER
1040 1080 3030 3040 3060

J - COUNTER
3050 3050

END OF VAR. LIST
```

Slow Print From Data

At times it is desirable to control the speed at which the computer places information on the screen. While some computers such as the Apple II have a SPEED command to accommodate such a situation, there are simple routines that can do the same thing on the other computers. The following routine will take lines from data statements and place them on the screen at a preset letter by letter pace (determined by SP). This technique is most useful when you want to present a mass of information without interruption. It should work without modification on most computers.

```
*******************************
*                             *
*     SLOW PRINT FROM DATA    *
*                             *
*           ORWIG             *
*******************************
```

```
10   REM   THIS IS A PROGRAM WHICH PRINTS AT A PRESET PACE
20   REM   FROM DATA STATEMENTS IN THE PROGRAM
100  REM   START OF MAIN PROGRAM
110  REM   SET SPEED
120  SP = 50
130  REM   GET A LINE TO PRINT
140  GOSUB 1020
150  REM   CHECK FOR END OF DATA
160  GOSUB 2010
170  REM   GET LENGTH OF LINE
180  GOSUB 3010
```

(continued)

```
190   REM   PRINT LINE
200   GOSUB 3040
210   REM   GET NEXT LINE
220   GOTO 130
230   REM   END OF MAIN PROGRAM
240   PRINT "THE END"
250   END
1000  REM   START OF SUBROUTINES
1010  REM   GET LINE FROM DATA
1020  READ A$
1030  RETURN
2000  REM   CHECK FOR END OF DATA
2010  IF A$ = "999" THEN 240
2020  RETURN
3000  REM   GET LENGTH OF LINE
3010 LE =  LEN (A$)
3020  RETURN
3030  REM   PRINT LINE
3040  FOR I = 1 TO LE
3050  PRINT  MID$ (A$,I,1);
3060  FOR J = 1 TO SP
3070  NEXT J
3080  NEXT I
3090  PRINT
3100  RETURN
4000  REM   DATA
4010  DATA   "THIS IS A SAMPLE OF SPEED CONTROLLED"
4020  DATA   "PRINTING.   IN THE PROGRAM THE VALUE"
4030  DATA   "OF SP DETERMINES THE SPEED OF PRINTING."
4040  DATA   "BE CAREFUL WITH COMMAS. SOME COMPUTERS"
4050  DATA   "GET CONFUSED BY THEM IN THIS KIND OF"
4060  DATA   "DATA STATEMENT - - ESPECIALLY IF YOU"
4070  DATA   "CAN'T USE THE QUOTE MARKS AT THE "
4080  DATA   "BEGINNING AND END OF EACH STATEMENT."
4090  REM   END FLAG
4100  DATA   "999"
```

```
******************************
*                            *
*    SLOW PRINT FROM DATA    *
*                            *
*   -->TABLE OF VARIABLES<-- *
*                            *
******************************
```

```
A$ - LINE TO PRINT
1020 2010 3010 3050

I - COUNTER
3040 3050 3080

J - COUNTER
3060 3070

LE - LENGTH OF LINE
3010 3040

SP - DELAY VALUE FOR SPEED
120 3060

END OF VAR. LIST
```

Slow Print from Data 2

The following program produces exactly the same effect as the earlier one. It demonstrates the process of incorporating the routines directly into the program. This is by far the most economical technique for working with routines that are not used repetitively in a program. However, it also makes it more difficult to develop a concept for what each routine actually does.

```
10 SP = 50
20   READ A$
30   IF A$ = "999" THEN   END
40 LE =  LEN (A$)
50   FOR I = 1 TO LE
60   PRINT  MID$ (A$,I,1);
70   FOR J = 1 TO SP
80   NEXT J
90   NEXT I
100   PRINT
110   GOTO 20
120   DATA  "THIS IS A SAMPLE OF SPEED CONTROLLED"
130   DATA  "PRINTING.  IN THE PROGRAM THE VALUE"
140   DATA  "OF SP DETERMINES THE SPEED OF PRINTING."
150   DATA  "BE CAREFUL WITH COMMAS. SOME COMPUTERS"
160   DATA  "GET CONFUSED BY THEM IN THIS KIND OF"
170   DATA  "DATA STATEMENT - - ESPECIALLY IF YOU"
180   DATA  "CAN'T USE THE QUOTE MARKS AT THE "
190   DATA  "BEGINNING AND END OF EACH STATEMENT."
200   DATA  "999"
```

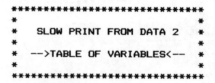

```
A$ - LINE TO PRINT
20 30 40 60

I - COUNTER
50 60 90
```

(continued)

```
J - COUNTER
70 80

LE - LENGTH OF LINE
40 50

SP - DELAY VALUE FOR SPEED
10 70

END OF VAR. LIST
```

Slow Print from Lines

At times it is better to print only selected lines at a reduced speed. These lines are often easiest to handle if they are incorporated into the body of the program, just as PRINT statements normally would be. The following routine demonstrates one technique for doing this. About the only unusual characteristic of this program is the use of two statements per line. Virtually all microcomputer BASIC languages allow this, as long as you use the appropriate symbol (usually a :) to separate the statements. With Apple II computer, consider using the SPEED command.

```
*******************************
*                             *
*    SLOW PRINT FROM LINES    *
*                             *
*            ORWIG            *
*******************************
```

```
10   REM   THIS IS A SPEED CONTROLLED PRINT PROGRAM
20   REM   WHICH PRINTS FROM LINES IN THE PROGRAM
100   REM   START OF MAIN PROGRAM
110   REM   SET PRINT SPEED
120 SP = 50
130   REM   THE LINE IS ASSIGNED TO VARIABLE A$
140   REM   THEN EACH LINE IS SENT TO THE PRINTING SUBROUTINE
150 A$ = "PRINTING THROUGH THE USE OF A SUB-": GOSUB 1010
160 A$ = "ROUTINE.": GOSUB 1010
170 A$ = "FOR CONVENIENCE, THE 'GOSUB' IS USUALLY": GOSUB 1010
180 A$ = "PLACED AT THE END OF EACH LINE": GOSUB 1010
190 A$ = "INSTEAD OF ON SEPARATE LINES.": GOSUB 1010
200   REM   END OF MAIN PROGRAM
210   END
1000   REM   START OF SUBROUTINE
1010   REM   SPEED CONTROL SUBROUTINE
1020 LE =   LEN (A$)
1030   FOR I = 1 TO LE
1040   PRINT  MID$ (A$,I,1); .
1050   FOR J = 1 TO SP
1060   NEXT J
1070   NEXT I
1080   PRINT
1090   RETURN
```

```
*******************************
*                             *
*    SLOW PRINT FROM LINES    *
*                             *
*   -->TABLE OF VARIABLES<--  *
*                             *
*******************************
```

```
A$ - LINE TO PRINT
150 160 170 180 190 1020 1040

I - COUNTER
1030 1040 1070

J - COUNTER
1050 1060

LE - LENGTH OF LINE
1020 1030

SP - DELAY VALUE FOR SPEED
120 1050

END OF VAR. LIST
```

Forward-Backward

There are frequent situations in instructional programs where you might want to build in the option of allowing the student to return to an earlier frame by simply pressing a designated key. For example, such a technique would allow a student to review an earlier frame quickly and easily if the going suddenly started to get tough. The only areas that will need modification for various computers are the GET statements.

```
*******************************
*                             *
*     FORWARD - BACKWARD      *
*                             *
*            ORWIG            *
*******************************
```

```
10   REM   THIS METHOD OF CONTROLLING FORWARD AND
20   REM   BACKWARD MOVEMENT THROUGH A PROGRAM USES
30   REM   GO TO STATEMENTS
100  REM   START OF MAIN PROGRAM
110  REM    BLOCK ONE
120  HOME
130  PRINT "THIS IS BLOCK ONE, FRAME 1"
```

(continued)

```
140    GOSUB 1010
150    PRINT "THIS IS BLOCK ONE, FRAME 2."
160    PRINT
170    PRINT
175    PRINT "TO KEEP THINGS SIMPLE,"
180    PRINT "YOU CAN PLACE ANY NUMBER OF FRAMES"
190    PRINT "IN EACH BLOCK, BUT YOU SHOULD ONLY GO"
200    PRINT "BACK TO THE BEGINNING OF EACH BLOCK."
210    GOSUB 1010
220    REM   BLOCK TWO
230    PRINT "THIS IS BLOCK TWO"
240    GOSUB 2000
250    IF SA$ = "B" THEN 110
260    REM   BLOCK THREE
270    PRINT "THIS IS BLOCK THREE"
280    GOSUB 2000
290    IF SA$ = "B" THEN 220
300    HOME
310    PRINT "FINISHED!"
320    REM   END OF MAIN PROGRAM
330    END
1000   REM   START OF SUBROUTINES
1010   REM   PRINT FORWARD ONLY MESSAGE
1020   VTAB 23
1030   PRINT "PRESS ANY KEY TO CONTINUE"
1040   GET SA$
1050   HOME
1060   RETURN
2000   REM   PRINT BACKWARD - FORWARD MESSAGE
2010   VTAB 22
2020   PRINT "PRESS 'B' TO GO BACK"
2030   PRINT "PRESS ANY KEY TO CONTINUE"
2040   GET SA$
2050   HOME
2060   RETURN
```

```
********************************
*                              *
*      FORWARD - BACKWARD      *
*                              *
*    -->TABLE OF VARIABLES<--  *
*                              *
********************************
```

SA$ - STORE KEY RESPONSE
250 290 1040 2040

END OF VAR. LIST

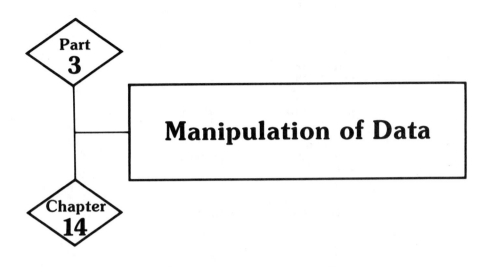

Part
3

Manipulation of Data

Chapter
14

Direct Use of Data

DATA statements can be extremely useful in instructional programs. Since you can locate all topical information in the DATA statements, you can repeatedly use one fundamental program just by changing the contents of those DATA statements. The following program demonstrates a simple application of DATA statements in a spelling program. Don't be put off by the simple nature of the spelling words. These words are called *dummy data* and are used to let you play with the program. Once you have it working, and understand it, you can change the DATA statements to include more challenging words. In this series of programs, the first data statement contains the number of problems. This value is read into N. If you change the number of problems, be sure to change the first DATA statement accordingly. Depending on your computer, you may have to change the HOME and VTAB commands to ones that your computer uses.

```
*******************************
*                             *
*      DIRECT USE OF DATA      *
*                             *
*            ORWIG             *
*******************************
```

```
10   REM  DIRECT ACCESS OF DATA STATEMENTS
100  REM   MAIN PROGRAM
110  REM   GET A PROBLEM
120  GOSUB 1010
130  REM     CHECK FOR END OF PROBLEMS
140  GOSUB 3000
150  REM    SHOW THE PROBLEM
160  GOSUB 4000
170  REM  ACCEPT AND CHECK ANSWER
180  GOSUB 5000
190  IF SC = 0 THEN 150
200  GOTO 110
210  REM   END OF MAIN PROGRAM
1000  REM   START OF SUBROUTINES
1010  REM   GET A PROBLEM
1020  READ A$
1030  RETURN
3000  REM  CHECK FOR END OF DATA
3010  IF A$ < > "999" THEN   RETURN
3020  PRINT "WE ARE FINISHED!"
3030  END
4000  REM   SHOW THE PROBLEM
4010  HOME
4020  VTAB 12
4030  PRINT "SPELL THIS WORD"
4040  FOR K = 1 TO 600
4050  NEXT K
4060  HOME
4070  VTAB 13
4080  PRINT A$
4090  FOR K = 1 TO 200
4100  NEXT K
4110  HOME
4120  VTAB 14
4130  RETURN
5000  REM   ACCEPT ANSWER
5010  INPUT SA$
5020  REM   JUDGE ANSWER
5030  IF SA$ = A$ THEN 5090
5040 SC = 0
5050  PRINT "THAT WAS NOT CORRECT.   TRY IT AGAIN."
5060  FOR K = 1 TO 800
5070  NEXT K
5080  RETURN
5090  REM   CORRECT ANSWER
5100 SC = 1
5110  PRINT "VERY GOOD!"
5120  FOR K = 1 TO 800
5130  NEXT K
5140  RETURN
10000  REM   START OF DATA
10010  DATA   "CAT","TREE","DOG","HOUSE","ROOF"
10020  DATA   "999"
10030  REM   END OF DATA
```

```
*******************************
*                             *
*      DIRECT USE OF DATA      *
*                             *
*    -->TABLE OF VARIABLES<--  *
*                             *
*******************************
```

A$ - SPELLING WORD
1020 3010 4080 5030

K - DELAY COUNTER
4040 4050 4090 4100 5060 5070 5120 5130

SA$ - STUDENT ANSWER
5010 5030

SC - RIGHT OR WRONG
190 5040 5100

END OF VAR. LIST

Multiple-Choice Array

An array can be extremely useful in instructional programming. Unfortunately, it can also be confusing. Briefly, you can think of an array as a special way of labeling a portion of your computer's random-access memory. Since a complete discussion of lists and arrays is beyond the scope of this book, I will leave further research to you. However, you don't have to understand them completely in order to use them. The following program shows a simple process of storing the information in the DATA statements into an array before the program uses the information. While this program does nothing that DATA statements alone couldn't do, we are taking small steps here. Later programs will expand on the power of arrays. The HOME, VTAB, and HTAB statements may need modification for your computer.

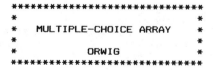

```
*******************************
*                             *
*    MULTIPLE-CHOICE ARRAY     *
*                             *
*            ORWIG             *
*******************************
```

```
10   REM  A PROGRAM TO DEMONSTRATE LOADING A TWO
20   REM  DIMENSION ARRAY.   IN THIS CASE THE
```

(continued)

```
30   REM   ARRAY WILL BE "N" BY 6.
1000   REM   MAIN PROGRAM
1010   REM   GET SIZE OF ARRAY
1020   READ N
1030   REM   DIMENSION ARRAY
1040   REM   NOT ALL COMPUTERS ALLOW VARS. IN DIM STATEMENTS.
1050   REM   IN THIS CASE, YOU WILL HAVE TO USE THE
1060   REM   LARGEST NUMBER YOU WOULD EXPECT TO HAVE.
1070   DIM A$(N,6)
1080   REM   READ DATA INTO ARRAY
1090   FOR I = 1 TO N
1100   FOR J = 1 TO 6
1110   READ A$(I,J)
1120   NEXT J
1130   NEXT I
2000   REM   USE ARRAYS
2010   FOR I = 1 TO N
2020   HOME
2030   VTAB 6
2040   REM   PRINT QUESTION
2050   PRINT A$(I,1)
2060   PRINT
2070   PRINT
2080   REM   PRINT NUMBERED CHOICES
2090   FOR J = 2 TO 5
2100   HTAB 10
2110   PRINT J - 1;".   ";A$(I,J)
2120   NEXT J
2130   PRINT
3000   REM   INPUT ANSWER
3010   GET SA$
3020   IF SA$ <  > A$(I,6) THEN 4000
3030   PRINT "VERY GOOD!"
3040   FOR K = 1 TO 800
3050   NEXT K
3060   NEXT I
3070   PRINT
3080   PRINT "FINISHED"
3090   END
4000   REM   WRONG ANSWER
4010   PRINT "SORRY, TRY AGAIN."
4020   FOR K = 1 TO 400
4030   NEXT K
4040   REM   PRINT SAME QUESTION
4050   GOTO 2020
5000   REM   DATA
5010   REM   THE FIRST DATA STATEMENT IS "N" - THE NUMBER OF QUESTIO
       NS
5020   DATA   3
5030   DATA   "WHAT IS THE MONTH AFTER JULY","JUNE","MARCH","AUGUST"
       ,"SEPTEMBER","3"
5040   DATA   "WHAT DAY COMES RIGHT AFTER FRIDAY?","SATURDAY","MONDA
       Y","SUNDAY","THURSDAY","1"
5050   DATA   "IN WHICH MONTH IS THANKSGIVING?","SEPTEMBER","DECEMBE
       R","JULY","NOVEMBER","4"
```

```
******************************
*                            *
*    MULTIPLE-CHOICE ARRAY    *
*                            *
*    -->TABLE OF VARIABLES<--  *
*                            *
******************************
```

A$(*,*) - DATA ARRAY
1070 1110 2050 2110 3020

I - COUNTER
1090 1110 1130 2010 2050 2110 3020 3060

J - COUNTER
1100 1110 1120 2090 2110 2110 2120

K - DELAY COUNTER
3040 3050 4020 4030

N - NUMBER OF PROBLEMS
1020 1070 1090 2010

SA$ - STUDENT ANSWER
3010 3020

END OF VAR. LIST

Sequential Data

One nice aspect of transfering DATA information to arrays is that it is easy to access any part of the array repeatedly if need be. This is not easy to do when you use only DATA and READ statements. The following program demonstrates the recycling of questions that were missed earlier. This is done by flagging the questions with a "C" if they have been answered correctly, and an "I" if they have been answered incorrectly. The program cycles through the questions until all of them have a "C." The HOME and VTAB commands may need to be modified for various computers.

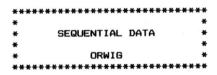

```
******************************
*                            *
*      SEQUENTIAL DATA        *
*                            *
*          ORWIG             *
******************************
```

10 REM SEQUENTIAL PRESENTATION WITH DATA IN ARRAY - - ALLOWS REP
    EAT OF MISSED PROBLEMS

(continued)

```
100   REM   MAIN PROGRAM
110   REM   LOAD ARRAY FROM DATA STATEMENTS
120   GOSUB 1010
130   REM   GET SEQUENCE NUMBER
140   GOSUB 2000
150   REM   CHECK FOR STATUS OF PROBLEM
160   IF A$(R,2) = "C" THEN 130
170   IF A$(R,2) = "I" THEN   GOSUB 3000
180   REM   PRESENT PROBLEM
190   GOSUB 4000
200   REM   CHECK THE ANSWER
210   GOSUB 5000
220   REM   NOT FINISHED, SO GO BACK TO GET ANOTHER PROBLEM
230   GOTO 130
240   REM   END OF MAIN PROGRAM
1000   REM   START OF SUBROUTINES
1010   REM   READ DATA INTO ARRAY
1020   READ N
1030   DIM A$(N,2)
1040   FOR I = 1 TO N
1050   READ A$(I,1)
1060 A$(I,2) = "N"
1070   NEXT I
1080   RETURN
2000   REM   SEQUENCING ROUTINE
2010   IF R = N THEN R = 0
2020 R = R + 1
2030   RETURN
3000   REM   THIS PROBLEM WAS MISSED EARLIER
3010   HOME
3020   VTAB 12
3030   PRINT "TRY THIS ONE AGAIN"
3040   FOR K = 1 TO 1000
3050   NEXT K
3060   RETURN
4000   REM   SHOW THE PROBLEM
4010   HOME
4020   VTAB 12
4030   PRINT "SPELL THIS WORD"
4040   FOR K = 1 TO 600
4050   NEXT K
4060   HOME
4070   VTAB 13
4080   PRINT A$(R,1)
4090   FOR K = 1 TO 200
4100   NEXT K
4110   HOME
4120   VTAB 14
4130   RETURN
5000   REM   ACCEPT ANSWER
5010   INPUT SA$
5020   REM   JUDGE ANSWER
5030   IF SA$ = A$(R,1) THEN 5100
5040 A$(R,2) = "I"
5050   PRINT "THAT WAS NOT CORRECT.   WE WILL TRY IT"
5060   PRINT "AGAIN LATER."
5070   FOR K = 1 TO 800
5080   NEXT K
5090   RETURN
5100   REM   CORRECT ANSWER
5110   PRINT "VERY GOOD!"
```

(continued)

```
5120  FOR K = 1 TO 800
5130  NEXT K
5140 A$(R,2) = "C"
6000  REM  CHECK FOR COMPLETION
6010 CR = CR + 1
6020  IF CR = N THEN 7000
6030  RETURN
7000  REM  FINISHED
7010  PRINT "WE ARE FINISHED!"
7020  END
10000  DATA  5
10010  DATA  "CAT","TREE","DOG","HOUSE","ROOF"
```

```
*******************************
*                             *
*       SEQUENTIAL DATA        *
*                             *
*    -->TABLE OF VARIABLES<--  *
*                             *
*******************************
```

```
A$(*,*) - DATA ARRAY
160 170 1030 1050 1060 4080 5030 5040 5140

CR - NUMBER CORRECT
6010 6010 6020

I - COUNTER
1040 1050 1060 1070

K - DELAY COUNTER
3040 3050 4040 4050 4090 4100 5070 5080 5120 5130

N - NUMBER OF PROBLEMS
1020 1030 1040 2010 6020

R - SEQUENCE NUMBER
160 170 2010 2010 2020 2020 4080 5030 5040 5140

SA$ - STUDENT ANSWER
5010 5030

END OF VAR. LIST
```

Random-Selection Array

Now we are getting to the good part. The following program loads the DATA statements into an array, then selects items from the array at random. It also checks to see if the problem has been missed earlier. This type of presentation is difficult if you don't use an array. In this program you may need to modify the HOME, VTAB, and RND commands.

```
*******************************
*                             *
*    RANDOM SELECTION ARRAY   *
*                             *
*           ORWIG             *
*******************************
```

```
10   REM   RANDOM SELECTION ARRAY
20   REM   WHICH MARKS CORRECT ANSWERS
100   REM   MAIN PROGRAM
110   REM   LOAD ARRAY FROM DATA STATEMENTS
120   GOSUB 1010
130   REM   GET A RANDOM NUMBER BETWEEN 1 AND N
140   GOSUB 2000
150   REM   CHECK FOR STATUS OF PROBLEM
160   IF A$(R,2) = "C" THEN 140
170   IF A$(R,2) = "I" THEN   GOSUB 3000
180   REM   PRESENT PROBLEM
190   GOSUB 4000
200   REM   CHECK THE ANSWER
210   GOSUB 5000
220   REM   NOT FINISHED, SO GO BACK TO GET ANOTHER PROBLEM
230   GOTO 130
240   REM   END OF MAIN PROGRAM
1000   REM   START OF SUBROUTINES
1010   REM   READ DATA INTO ARRAY
1020   READ N
1030   DIM A$(N,2)
1040   FOR I = 1 TO N
1050   READ A$(I,1)
1060   A$(I,2) = "N"
1070   NEXT I
1080   RETURN
2000   REM   RANDOMIZING ROUTINE
2010   R =   INT ( RND (1) * N) + 1
2020   RETURN
3000   REM   THIS PROBLEM WAS MISSED EARLIER
3010   HOME
3020   VTAB 12
3030   PRINT "TRY THIS ONE AGAIN"
3040   FOR K = 1 TO 1000
3050   NEXT K
3060   RETURN
4000   REM   SHOW THE PROBLEM
4010   HOME
4020   VTAB 12
4030   PRINT "SPELL THIS WORD"
4040   FOR K = 1 TO 600
4050   NEXT K
4060   HOME
4070   VTAB 13
4080   PRINT A$(R,1)
4090   FOR K = 1 TO 200
4100   NEXT K
4110   HOME
4120   VTAB 14
4130   RETURN
5000   REM   ACCEPT ANSWER
5010   INPUT SA$
```

(continued)

```
5020   REM   JUDGE ANSWER
5030   IF SA$ = A$(R,1) THEN 5100
5040 A$(R,2) = "I"
5050   PRINT "THAT WAS NOT CORRECT.   WE WILL TRY IT"
5060   PRINT "AGAIN LATER."
5070   FOR K = 1 TO 800
5080   NEXT K
5090   RETURN
5100   REM   CORRECT ANSWER
5110   PRINT "VERY GOOD!"
5120 A$(R,2) = "C"
5130   FOR K = 1 TO 800
5140   NEXT K
6000   REM   CHECK TO SEE IF FINISHED
6010 CO = 0
6020   FOR L = 1 TO N
6030   IF A$(L,2) = "C" THEN CO = CO + 1
6040   NEXT L
6050   IF CO <  > N THEN   RETURN
6060   PRINT "WE ARE FINISHED!"
6070   END
10000   DATA  5
10010   DATA   "CAT","TREE","DOG","HOUSE","ROOF"
```

```
******************************
*                            *
*    RANDOM SELECTION ARRAY   *
*                            *
*   -->TABLE OF VARIABLES<--  *
*                            *
******************************
```

A$(*,*) - DATA ARRAY
160 170 1030 1050 1060 4080 5030 5040 5120 6030

CO - PROBLEMS CORRECT
6010 6030 6030 6050

I - COUNTER
1040 1050 1060 1070

K - DELAY COUNTER
3040 3050 4040 4050 4090 4100 5070 5080 5130 5140

L - COUNTER
6020 6030 6040

N - NUMBER OF PROBLEMS
1020 1030 1040 2010 6020 6050

R - RANDOM NUMBER
160 170 2010 4080 5030 5040 5120

SA$ - STUDENT ANSWER
5010 5030

END OF VAR. LIST

Shrinking List

A true programmer might sneer at the earlier program because it is not efficient. Once a problem has been answered correctly, it is no longer needed. The earlier program kept all the problems and had to check constantly through all of them to see if any were unfinished. For a large number of problems (say, 50 or 60), this could be inefficient. It might even cause delays of several seconds. This program solves that problem. It simply pitches out the questions that have been correctly answered, so it needs to deal only with those that have not been asked and those that have been answered incorrectly. This is a better way to write such a program. Several seconds here and there can indeed become time-consuming. For you non-Apple people, you may need to modify the HOME, VTAB, and RND statements.

```
10   REM     RANDOM PRESENTATION OF AN ARRAY WHICH DROPS OUT CORRECT
          ANSWERS
100  REM   MAIN PROGRAM
110  REM   LOAD ARRAY FROM DATA STATEMENTS
120  GOSUB 1010
130  REM   GET A RANDOM NUMBER BETWEEN 1 AND N
140  GOSUB 2000
150  REM   CHECK FOR STATUS OF PROBLEM
160  IF A$(R,2) = "I" THEN   GOSUB 3000
170  REM   PRESENT PROBLEM
180  GOSUB 4000
190  REM   CHECK THE ANSWER
200  GOSUB 5000
210  REM   NOT FINISHED, SO GO BACK TO GET ANOTHER PROBLEM
220  GOTO 130
230  REM   END OF MAIN PROGRAM
1000  REM   START OF SUBROUTINES
1010  REM   READ DATA INTO ARRAY
1020  READ N
1030  DIM A$(N,2)
1040  FOR I = 1 TO N
1050  READ A$(I,1)
1060 A$(I,2) = "N"
1070  NEXT I
1080  RETURN
2000  REM   RANDOMIZING ROUTINE
2010 R =   INT ( RND (1) * N) + 1
2020  RETURN
3000  REM   THIS PROBLEM WAS MISSED EARLIER
3010  HOME
3020  VTAB 12
```

(continued)

```
3030   PRINT "TRY THIS ONE AGAIN"
3040   FOR K = 1 TO 1000
3050   NEXT K
3060   RETURN
4000   REM   SHOW THE PROBLEM
4010   HOME
4020   VTAB 12
4030   PRINT "SPELL THIS WORD"
4040   FOR K = 1 TO 600
4050   NEXT K
4060   HOME
4070   VTAB 13
4080   PRINT A$(R,1)
4090   FOR K = 1 TO 200
4100   NEXT K
4110   HOME
4120   VTAB 14
4130   RETURN
5000   REM   ACCEPT ANSWER
5010   INPUT SA$
5020   REM   JUDGE ANSWER
5030   IF SA$ = A$(R,1) THEN 5100
5040   A$(R,2) = "I"
5050   PRINT "THAT WAS NOT CORRECT.   WE WILL TRY IT"
5060   PRINT "AGAIN LATER."
5070   FOR K = 1 TO 800
5080   NEXT K
5090   RETURN
5100   REM   CORRECT ANSWER
5110   PRINT "VERY GOOD!"
5120   FOR K = 1 TO 800
5130   NEXT K
6000   REM    RESTACK THE ARRAY AND CHECK TO SEE IF DONE
6010   REM    PLACE BOTTOM PROBLEM IN ARRAY INTO POSITION OF ONE JUST
       ANSWERED CORRECTLY, THEN DECREASE SIZE OF ACTIVE ARRAY BY ON
    E
6020   A$(R,1) = A$(N,1)
6030   A$(R,2) = A$(N,2)
6040   N = N - 1
6050   IF N < > 0 THEN   RETURN
6060   PRINT "WE ARE FINISHED!"
6070   END
10000   DATA   5
10010   DATA   "CAT","TREE","DOG","HOUSE","ROOF"
```

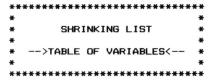

```
******************************
*                            *
*        SHRINKING LIST      *
*                            *
*    -->TABLE OF VARIABLES<-- *
*                            *
******************************
```

```
A$(*,*) - DATA ARRAY
160 1030 1050 1060 4080 5030 5040 6020 6020 6030 6030
```

(continued)

I - COUNTER
1040 1050 1060 1070

K - DELAY COUNTER
3040 3050 4040 4050 4090 4100 5070 5080 5120 5130

N - NUMBER OF PROBLEMS
1020 1030 1040 2010 6020 6030 6040 6040 6050

R - RANDOM NUMBER
160 2010 4080 5030 5040 6020 6030

SA$ - STUDENT ANSWER
5010 5030

END OF VAR. LIST

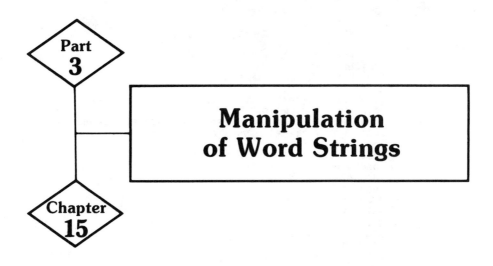

Part 3

Manipulation of Word Strings

Chapter 15

Alphabetize

There are times when you might need to alphabetize a set of words. This might be used to check a student's effort at alphabetizing, or it might simply be used to return a list of words in an organized form. Although the following routine might look confusing, it isn't. The words are stored in an array, then the "largest" words (those highest in the alphabet) are gradually sifted to the bottom of the array. This program should work on any microcomputer that can use dimensioned string arrays.

```
*****************************
*                           *
*        ALPHABETIZE        *
*                           *
*          ORWIG            *
*****************************
```

```
10   REM   THIS IS A SET OF ROUTINES WHICH WILL ALPH. A LIST OF WORD
     S
100  REM   START MAIN PROGRAM
```

(continued)

```
110   REM   SET DIM A$() TO THE MAXIMUM NUMBER OF WORDS YOU WILL HAV
      E
120   DIM A$(100)
130   REM   GET ORIGINAL LIST
140   GOSUB 1010
150   REM   ALPH. THE LIST
160   GOSUB 2000
170   REM   PRINT OUT THE FINISHED LIST
180   GOSUB 3000
190   REM   END OF MAIN PROGRAM
200   END
1000  REM   START OF SUBROUTINES
1010  REM   GET WORDS
1020  PRINT "TYPE EACH WORD, FOLLOWED BY 'RETURN'.
1030  PRINT "TYPE IN 999 TO FINISH."
1040  INPUT SA$
1050  IF SA$ = "999" THEN   RETURN
1060  N = N + 1
1070  A$(N) = SA$
1080  GOTO 1040
2000  REM   ALPH. THE LIST
2010  FOR I = 1 TO N
2020  FOR J = 1 TO N - I
2030  A$ = A$(J)
2040  B$ = A$(J + 1)
2050  IF A$ < B$ THEN 2080
2060  A$(J) = B$
2070  A$(J + 1) = A$
2080  NEXT J
2090  NEXT I
2100  RETURN
3000  REM   PRINT OUT ALPH. LIST
3010  PRINT
3020  FOR I = 1 TO N
3030  PRINT A$(I)
3040  NEXT I
3050  RETURN
```

```
*******************************
*                             *
*          ALPHABETIZE        *
*                             *
*     -->TABLE OF VARIABLES<-- *
*                             *
*******************************
```

A$ - ONE WORD IN LIST
2030 2050 2070

A$(*) - WORD LIST
120 1070 2030 2040 2060 2070 3030

B$ - NEXT WORD IN LIST
2040 2050 2060

I - COUNTER
2010 2020 2090 3020 3030 3040

(continued)

```
J - COUNTER
2020 2030 2040 2060 2070 2080

N - NUMBER OF WORDS
1060 1060 1070 2010 2020 3020

SA$ - WORDS TYPED IN
1040 1050 1070

END OF VAR. LIST
```

Word Shuffle

A number of vocabulary games and instructional units can utilize word "mixing" routines. You can start with normal words, but you end with words whose letters have been mixed to some extent. In this particular routine, the value of R1 determines how many times the word is shuffled, and the value of R2 determines which letter is pulled from the middle of the word. Adjusting these values will give varying degrees of shuffling. This program will need the RND functions adjusted for various computers.

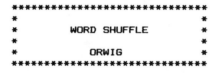

```
******************************
*                            *
*        WORD SHUFFLE        *
*                            *
*           ORWIG            *
******************************
```

```
10   REM   A PROGRAM TO RANDOMLY REARRANGE THE LETTERS IN A WORD.
100    REM    MAIN PROGRAM
110    REM    GET A WORD
120    GOSUB 1000
130    REM    GET ITS LENGTH
140    GOSUB 2000
150    REM    RANDOMIZE THE WORD
160    GOSUB 5000
170    GOSUB 3000
180    REM    PRINT THE WORD
190    GOSUB 4000
200    REM    END OF MAIN PROGRAM
210    END
1000   REM    INPUT A WORD
1010   PRINT "TYPE IN A WORD"
1020    INPUT A$
1030 B$ = A$
1040    RETURN
2000   REM    GET LENGTH OF WORD
2010 A =   LEN (A$)
2020    RETURN
3000   REM    MIX UP THE WORD
```

(continued)

```
3010   FOR I = 1 TO R1
3020    GOSUB 6000
3030    REM   THE FOLLOWING LINE PULLS A LETTER FROM THE MIDDLE OF TH
       E WORD AND PUTS IT AT THE FRONT
3040 B$ =  MID$ (B$,R2,1) +  MID$ (B$,1,R2 - 1) +  MID$ (B$,R2 + 1
       ,A - R2)
3050    NEXT I
3060    RETURN
4000    REM   PRINT MIXED UP WORD
4010    PRINT A$
4020    PRINT B$
4030    RETURN
5000    REM   ONE RANDOM NUMBER
5010    REM   DETERMINES THE NUMBER OF TIMES THE WORD IS SHUFFLED.   T
       HE BIGGER R1 IS THE MORE SHUFFLED THE WORD BECOMES.
5020 R1 =   INT ( RND (1) * 25) + 1
5030    RETURN
6000    REM   ANOTHER RANDOM NUMBER
6010    REM   DETERMINES WHICH LETTER IS SHUFFLED
6020 R2 =   INT ( RND (1) * A) + 1
6030    RETURN
```

```
*******************************
*                             *
*        WORD SHUFFLE         *
*                             *
*    -->TABLE OF VARIABLES<--  *
*                             *
*******************************
```

```
A - LENGTH OF WORD
2010  3040  6020

A$ - WORD
1020  1030  2010  4010

B$ - SHUFFLED WORD
1030  3040  3040  3040  3040  4020

I - COUNTER
3010  3050

R1 - NUMBER OF SHUFFLES
3010  5020

R2 - LETTER SHUFFLED
3040  3040  3040  3040  6020

END OF VAR. LIST
```

Word-Scramble Array

The following routine goes a bit further with the word shuffling process. The individual letters of the word are stored in an array, and then the "string" is reassembled in a random pattern. With this method any letter in the word is likely to fall any place in the reconstructed string. This can make for very mixed-up words. The RND function might need to be adjusted for various computers.

```
*******************************
*                             *
*      WORD-SCRAMBLE ARRAY    *
*                             *
*            ORWIG            *
*******************************
```

```
10   REM   WORD SCRAMBLING ROUTINE USING A STRING ARRAY
100   REM    MAIN PROGRAM
110   REM    DIMENSION B$ TO TO LARGEST WORD YOU WOULD USE
120   DIM B$(25)
130   REM   GET A WORD
140   GOSUB 1010
150   REM   GET LENGTH OF WORD
160   GOSUB 2000
170   REM   RANDOMIZE WORD
180   GOSUB 3000
190   REM   PRINT THE WORD
200   GOSUB 4000
210   END
220   REM   END OF MAIN PROGRAM
1000   REM    START OF SUBROUTINES
1010   REM   GET A WORD
1020   PRINT "TYPE IN A WORD"
1030   INPUT A$
1040   RETURN
2000   REM   GET LENGTH OF WORD
2010 A =   LEN (A$)
2020   RETURN
3000   REM    RANDOMIZING SUBROUTINE
3010   REM    THE NEXT LINE CLEARS OUT ANY LEFTOVERS WHICH MIGHT BE I
       N D$
3020 D$ = ""
3030   REM    THE NEXT THREE LINES FILL B$()WITH 'EMPTY' FLAGS
3040   FOR I = 1 TO A
3050 B$(I) = "#"
3060   NEXT I
3070   REM    THE NEXT LINES FILL B$() AT RANDOM WITH LETTERS FROM TH
       E WORD
3080   FOR I = 1 TO A
3090 C$ =   MID$ (A$,I,1)
3100 R =   INT ( RND (1) * A) + 1
3110   IF B$(R) = "#" THEN 3130
3120   GOTO 3100
3130 B$(R) = C$
3140   NEXT I
3150   REM    THE NEXT LINES REASSEMBLE THE MIXED LETTERS INTO A 'WOR
       D'.
3160   FOR I = 1 TO A
3170 D$ = D$ + B$(I)
3180   NEXT I
3190   RETURN
```

(continued)

```
4000   REM   PRINT  THE  WORD
4010   PRINT  "HERE  IS  THE  SCRAMBLED  WORD."
4020   PRINT
4030   PRINT  D$
4040   RETURN
```

```
*******************************
*                             *
*      WORD-SCRAMBLE  ARRAY    *
*                             *
*    -->TABLE  OF  VARIABLES<--   *
*                             *
*******************************
```

```
A - LENGTH  OF  WORD
2010  3040  3080  3100  3160

A$ - WORD
1030  2010  3090

B$(*) - WORD  LETTER  ARRAY
120  3050  3110  3130  3170

C$ - ONE  LETTER  OF  WORD
3090  3130

D$ - SCRAMBLED  WORD
3020  3170  3170  4030

I - COUNTER
3040  3050  3060  3080  3090  3140  3160  3170  3180

R - RANDOM  NUMBER
3100  3110  3130

END  OF  VAR.  LIST
```

Easy Code

Kids seem to love codes, and codes can be used to help with the development of many skills. The least complicated codes "adjust" each letter in the alphabet by some predetermined amount. For example, if the key were "2", then "A" would become "C", "B" would become "D", and so on. It is easy to use the computer to build codes by using the ASC and CHR$ functions. The ASC function converts a letter into its ASCII numeric equivalent. This number can be adjusted by the key; then the CHR$ function converts it back into the new letter. This particular program catches punctuation and spaces and then passes them straight through. This process makes the code much less difficult to work with. There are several potential problem areas in this program when you start using it on other computers. Different computers sometimes produce different

ASCII codes. If yours does, you might need to make some modifications. Also, the GET statement varies from computer to computer.

```
*******************************
*                             *
*           EASY CODE         *
*                             *
*             ORWIG           *
*******************************
```

```
10   REM   A CODING PROGRAM
100    REM    START OF MAIN PROGRAM
110    REM    GET COMBINATION
120    GOSUB 1010
130    REM   GET ENCODE OR DECODE
140    GOSUB 2000
150    REM   GET THE MESSAGE
160    GOSUB 3000
170    REM   ENCODE / DECODE THE MESSAGE
180    GOSUB 4000
190    REM   PRINT THE MESSAGE
200    GOSUB 5000
210    REM   END OF MAIN PROGRAM
220    END
1000   REM    START OF SUBROUTINES
1010   REM   GET COMBINATION
1020   PRINT "TYPE IN YOUR COMBINATION"
1030   PRINT "USE ONE SMALL (LESS THAN 30) NUMBER. "
1040   REM    N IS THE AMOUNT BY WHICH EACH CHARACTER WILL BE CHANGE
       D
1050   INPUT N
1060   RETURN
2000   REM   ENCODE OR DECODE
2010   PRINT
2020   PRINT
2030   PRINT "DO YOU WANT TO:"
2040   PRINT
2050   PRINT "     1. ENCODE"
2060   PRINT "     2. DECODE"
2070   PRINT
2080   PRINT "SELECT ONE"
2090   GET SA$
2100   IF SA$ = "1" THEN 2150
2110   IF SA$ = "2" THEN 2140
2120   GOTO 2090
2130   REM   THE FOLLOWING LINE REVERSES THE COMBINATION FOR DECODIN
       G
2140   N =  - N
2150   RETURN
3000   REM   GET THE MESSAGE
3010   SA$ = ""
3020   PRINT "TYPE IN THE MESSAGE"
3030   REM   THE FOLLOWING IS USED INSTEAD OF AN 'INPUT' TO ALLOW CO
       MMAS TO BE TYPED IN WITHOUT CREATING CONFUSION IN THE COMPUTE
       R.
```

(*continued*)

```
3040   GET S$
3050   IF   ASC (S$) = 13 THEN 3090
3060   PRINT S$;
3070  SA$ = SA$ + S$
3080   GOTO 3040
3090   PRINT
3100   RETURN
4000   REM   ENCODE / DECODE
4010   REM   GET LENGTH OF MESSAGE
4020  L =   LEN (SA$)
4030   FOR I = 1 TO L
4040   REM   GET THE 'I'TH LETTER
4050  A$ =   MID$ (SA$,I,1)
4060   REM    GET THE ASCII DECIMAL VALUE FOR THE 'I'TH LETTER
4070  A =   ASC (A$)
4080   REM   THE NEXT LINES 'PASSES THROUGH' PUNCTUATION
4090   IF A < 65 OR A > 90 THEN 4160
4100   REM   ADD 'N' TO THE ASCII VALUE OF THE LETTER
4110  A = A + N
4120   REM    THE NEXT TWO LINES KEEP THE CODE WITHIN THE RANGE OF A
       LPHABET CHARACTERS FOR THE APPLE II
4130   IF A > 90 THEN A = A - 26: GOTO 4130
4140   IF A < 65 THEN A = A + 26: GOTO 4140
4150   REM   THE NEXT LINE GETS THE CHARACTER WHICH MATCHES THE NEW
       ASCII VALUE OF 'A'
4160  A$ =   CHR$ (A)
4170   REM   THE NEXT LINE BUILDS THE MESSAGE CHARACTER BY CHARACTER
       INTO B$
4180  B$ = B$ + A$
4190   NEXT I
4200   RETURN
5000   REM   PRINT MESSAGE
5010   PRINT
5020   PRINT B$
5030   RETURN
```

```
*******************************
*                             *
*         EASY CODE           *
*                             *
*   -->TABLE OF VARIABLES<--   *
*                             *
*******************************
```

```
A - ASCII VALUE OF A$
4070 4090 4090 4110 4110 4130 4130 4130 4140 4140 4140
4160

A$ - ONE LETTER OF MESSAGE
4050 4070 4160 4180

B$ - NEW MESSAGE
4180 4180 5020

I - COUNTER
4030 4050 4190
```

(continued)

```
L - LENGTH OF MESSAGE
4020 4030

N - KEY
1050 2140 2140 4110

S$ - EACH KEY PRESSED
3040 3050 3060 3070

SA$ - STUDENT ANSWER
2090 2100 2110 3010 3070 3070 4020 4050

END OF VAR. LIST
```

Tough Code

Here is a code program for professionals. Like the "easy code" program, this one shifts individual letters of the alphabet. Unlike the earlier program, this one uses three separate keys to mix the letters. The first key determines an initial "shift" in the alphabet. The second key determines how many letters will pass before an additional shift will occur, and the third key determines the amount of the additional shift. On top of this, all punctuation and spacing are coded. I can't think of many instructional applications for such a program, but it is fun to play with. Once again, you will have to follow the same alternate-computer precautions as with the "easy code" program.

```
******************************
*                            *
*          TOUGH CODE        *
*                            *
*            ORWIG           *
******************************
```

```
10   REM   A FAIRLY ADVANCED CODING PROGRAM
100   REM   START OF MAIN PROGRAM
110   REM   GET COMBINATION
120   GOSUB 1010
130   REM   GET ENCODE OR DECODE
140   GOSUB 2000
150   REM   GET THE MESSAGE
160   GOSUB 3000
170   REM   ENCODE / DECODE THE MESSAGE
180   GOSUB 4000
190   REM   PRINT THE MESSAGE
200   GOSUB 5000
210   REM   END OF MAIN PROGRAM
220   END
1000   REM   START OF SUBROUTINES
```

(continued)

```
1010    REM   GET COMBINATION
1020    PRINT "TYPE IN YOUR COMBINATION"
1030    PRINT "LIKE 2,3,4.   USE THREE SMALL NUMBERS"
1040    PRINT "SEPARATED WITH TWO COMMAS."
1050    REM  N IS THE INITIAL AMOUNT BY WHICH EACH CHARACTER WILL BE
        CHANGED
1060    REM  EACH 'O'TH CHARACTER WILL HAVE AN ADDITIONAL AMOUNT OF
        'P' CHANGE
1070    INPUT N,O,P
1080    IF O <  > O THEN 1150
1090    PRINT "UNAUTHORIZED ENTRY!!"
1100    PRINT "CALL THE POLICE!!"
1110    PRINT "JUST KIDDING, OF COURSE!   THE SECOND"
1120    PRINT "NUMBER CAN'T BE A O SINCE IT IS USED"
1130    PRINT "FOR DIVISION.   TRY AGAIN."
1140    GOTO 1020
1150    RETURN
2000    REM   ENCODE OR DECODE
2010    PRINT
2020    PRINT
2030    PRINT "DO YOU WANT TO:"
2040    PRINT
2050    PRINT "      1. ENCODE"
2060    PRINT "      2. DECODE"
2070    PRINT
2080    PRINT "SELECT ONE"
2090    GET SA$
2100    IF SA$ = "1" THEN 2150
2110    IF SA$ = "2" THEN 2140
2120    GOTO 2090
2130    REM  THE FOLLOWING LINE REVERSES THE COMBINATION FOR DECODIN
        G
2140 N =  - N:O =  - O:P =  - P
2150    RETURN
3000    REM   GET THE MESSAGE
3010 SA$ = ""
3020    PRINT "TYPE IN THE MESSAGE"
3030    REM  THE FOLLOWING IS USED INSTEAD OF AN 'INPUT' TO ALLOW CO
        MMAS TO BE TYPED IN WITHOUT CREATING CONFUSION IN THE COMPUTE
        R.
3040    GET S$
3050    IF  ASC (S$) = 13 THEN 3090
3060    PRINT S$;
3070 SA$ = SA$ + S$
3080    GOTO 3040
3090    PRINT
3100    RETURN
4000    REM   ENCODE / DECODE
4010    REM   GET LENGTH OF MESSAGE
4020 L =  LEN (SA$)
4030    FOR I = 1 TO L
4040    REM    THE NEXT LINE DETERMINES THE VARIATION FOR EACH LETTER
        OF THE MESSAGE
4050    IF I / O =  INT (I / O) THEN N = N + P
4060    REM   GET THE 'I'TH LETTER
4070 A$ =  MID$ (SA$,I,1)
4080    REM    GET THE ASCII DECIMAL VALUE FOR THE 'I'TH LETTER
4090 A =  ASC (A$) + N
4100    REM  THE NEXT TWO LINES KEEP THE CODE WITHIN THE RANGE OF 'P
        RINTABLE' CHARACTERS FOR THE APPLE II
4110    IF A > 90 THEN A = A - 59: GOTO 4110
```

(continued)

```
4120   IF A < 32 THEN A = A + 59: GOTO 4120
4130   REM   THE NEXT LINE GETS THE CHARACTER WHICH MATCHES THE ASCI
       I VALUE OF A
4140   A$ =   CHR$ (A)
4150   REM   THE NEXT LINE BUILDS THE MESSAGE CHARACTER BY CHARACTER
       INTO B$
4160   B$ = B$ + A$
4170   NEXT I
4180   RETURN
5000   REM   PRINT MESSAGE
5010   PRINT
5020   PRINT B$
5030   RETURN
```

```
******************************
*                            *
*         TOUGH CODE         *
*                            *
*    -->TABLE OF VARIABLES<-- *
*                            *
******************************
```

A - ASCII VALUE OF A$
4090 4110 4110 4110 4120 4120 4120 4140

A$ - ONE LETTER OF MESSAGE
4070 4090 4140 4160

B$ - NEW MESSAGE
4160 4160 5020

I - COUNTER
4030 4050 4050 4070 4170

L - LENGTH OF MESSAGE
4020 4030

N - KEY 1
1070 2140 2140 4050 4050 4090

O - KEY 2
1070 1080 2140 2140 4050 4050

P - KEY 3
1070 2140 2140 4050

S$ - EACH KEYBOARD KEY PRESSED
3040 3050 3060 3070

SA$ - STUDENT ANSWER
2090 2100 2110 3010 3070 3070 4020 4070

END OF VAR. LIST

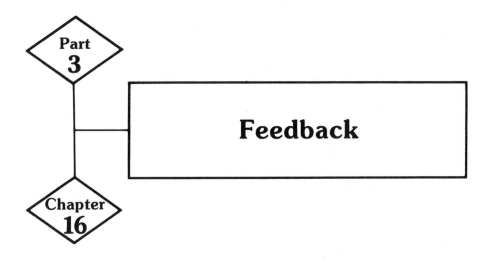

Part
3

Chapter
16

Feedback

Varied Feedback

While feedback is important in instruction, it can be irritating to see the same "Very good, Jennifer!" several dozen times in one lesson. To the greatest extent possible, feedback should be short, informative, and varied. If you want to get into graphics, this is an ideal place to get started. Unfortunately I won't discuss graphics in this book. As mentioned, there are too many variations among computers to make any discussion worthwhile. The only caution in the area of feedback is that you should avoid flashy wrong answer messages. You do not want to encourage learners to make incorrect selections merely so they can see the "fireworks." The following subroutines consider many of the aspects of appropriate feedback. They have been placed into one demonstration program, which can be run repeatedly until you understand what is happening. The most significant commands are the ON-GOTO's. These allow the diversity of responses. Obviously you can expand these to allow even more diversity. The HOME, VTAB, and RND statements will need modification for various computers. Also, before you go through a lot of trouble typing this in, you should make certain that your computer will accept the ON-GOTO command. Some earlier BASIC versions did not allow it.

```
*******************************
*                             *
*        VARIED FEEDBACK      *
*                             *
*           ORWIG             *
*******************************
```

```
10    REM   THIS IS A SAMPLE OF A PROGRAM WHICH USES SUBROUTINES TO P
      ROVIDE A VARIETY OF RIGHT AND WRONG ANSWER FEEDBACK.
100   REM   START OF MAIN PROGRAM
110   REM   SET A TIME FOR DISPLAY DELAY
120 DE = 1000
130   HOME
140   REM   MOVE DOWN THE SCREEN A WAYS
150   VTAB 5
160   PRINT "WHAT IS YOUR NAME?"
170   INPUT NA$
180   REM   ASK A QUESTION
190   GOSUB 1010
200   REM   JUDGE ANSWER
210   GOSUB 2000
220   REM   PROVIDE FEEDBACK
230   REM   GO GET A RANDOM NUMBER
240   GOSUB 6000
250   REM   DEPENDING ON VALUE OF SC, RIGHT OR WRONG FEEDBACK WILL B
      E DISPLAYED
260   ON SC GOSUB 3000,4000
270   GOSUB 5000
280   REM   IF ANSWER WAS WRONG, GO BACK.
290   IF SC = 2 GOTO 190
300   REM   END OF MAIN PROGRAM
310   END
1000  REM   START OF SUBROUTINES
1010  REM   ASK A QUESTION
1020  HOME
1030  VTAB 8
1040  PRINT
1050  PRINT NA$;", WHAT IS THE ANSWER TO THE"
1060  PRINT "FOLLOWING QUESTION?"
1070  PRINT
1080  PRINT "IN WHAT YEAR DID FLORIDA BECOME A STATE?"
1090  PRINT "      1. 1840
1100  PRINT "      2. 1845
1110  PRINT "      3. 1861
1120  PRINT "      4. 1868
1130  PRINT
1140  GET SA$
1150 C$ = "2"
1160  RETURN
2000  REM   JUDGE ANSWER
2010 SC = 2
2020  IF SA$ = C$ THEN SC = 1
2030  RETURN
3000  REM   REWARDS
3010  PRINT
3020  ON R GOTO 3040,3060,3080,3100,3120
3030  REM   REWARDS
3040  PRINT "GREAT!"
3050  RETURN
```

(continued)

```
3060   PRINT "SUPER!"
3070   RETURN
3080   PRINT "FANTASTIC!"
3090   RETURN
3100   PRINT "YOU'RE REALLY GOING NOW, ";NA$
3110   RETURN
3120   PRINT "THAT'S GREAT, ";NA$
3130   RETURN
4000   REM     WRONG
4010   ON R GOTO 4030,4050,4070,4090,4110
4020   REM   WRONGS
4030   PRINT "OOPS!"
4040   RETURN
4050   PRINT "LOOK CLOSER, ";NA$
4060   RETURN
4070   PRINT "NO...."
4080   RETURN
4090   PRINT "ARE YOU PAYING ATTENTION, ";NA$
4100   RETURN
4110   PRINT "SORRY!"
4120   RETURN
5000   REM   DELAY
5010   FOR I = 1 TO DE
5020   NEXT I
5030   RETURN
6000   REM   CALCULATE A RANDOM NUMBER
6010 R =   INT (5 *   RND (1)) + 1
6020   RETURN
```

```
*****************************
*                           *
*      VARIED FEEDBACK      *
*                           *
*   -->TABLE OF VARIABLES<-- *
*                           *
*****************************
```

C$ - CORRECT ANSWER
1150 2020

DE - DELAY VALUE
120 5010

I - COUNTER
5010 5020

NA$ - STUDENT'S NAME
170 1050 3100 3120 4050 4090

R - RANDOM NUMBER
3020 4010 6010

SA$ - STUDENT ANSWER
1140 2020

SC - SCORE
260 290 2010 2020

END OF VAR. LIST

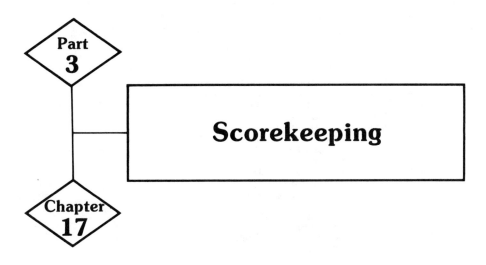

Part 3

Scorekeeping

Chapter 17

Score Reporter

The process of keeping scores can serve two purposes. First, it can keep the student informed of progress. Scores of this type are usually reported at the end of each unit of instruction. Second, the scores can keep the instructor informed of progress. These scores are usually kept on the program disk itself. In this way the instructor can review the progress of a number of students at a time when the students aren't using the computer. The first program presented in this section introduces the use of a *counter* to keep track of scores. If you look at the counter routines in lines 7020 and 7040, you might discover that they are not good "algebra" in that the two sides of the equations don't balance. Don't let this bother you. The computer interprets such lines as "Take the original value of Q, add 1 to it, then store the new value back in Q again." Thus the value of Q (or SC) increases by one each time that the computer goes through the appropriate line. Once again, for different computers you will have to modify the HOME and VTAB commands.

```
*******************************
*                             *
*        SCORE REPORTER       *
*                             *
*           ORWIG             *
*******************************
```

```
10   REM   A SIMPLE SCORING ROUTINE
100  REM    START OF MAIN PROGRAM
150  REM    GET QUESTION
160  GOSUB 3000
170  REM    CHECK FOR END OF QUESTIONS
180  IF Q$ = "999" THEN   GOTO 310
190  REM    SHOW QUESTION
200  GOSUB 4000
210  REM    ACCEPT ANSWER
220  GOSUB 5000
230  REM   JUDGE ANSWER
240  GOSUB 6000
250  REM   KEEP SCORE
260  GOSUB 7000
270  REM   PROVIDE FEEDBACK
280  GOSUB 8000
290  REM   GO BACK FOR ANOTHER QUESTION
300  GOTO 160
310  REM    PRESENT SCORE
320  GOSUB 12000
350  REM    END OF MAIN PROGRAM
360  END
1000   REM    START OF ROUTINES
2000   REM    RESERVED FOR LATER DEVELOPMENT
3000   REM    GET QUESTION
3010   READ Q$,A$
3020   RETURN
4000   REM    SHOW THE QUESTION
4010   HOME
4020   PRINT "             TRUE OR FALSE?"
4030   VTAB 10
4040   PRINT Q$
4050   PRINT
4060   RETURN
5000   REM   GET STUDENT'S ANSWER
5010   GET SA$
5020   REM MAKE CERTAIN IT IS A 'T' OR AN 'F'
5030   IF SA$ < > "T" AND SA$ < > "F" THEN   GOTO 5010
5040   RETURN
6000   REM   JUDGE ANSWER
6010   REM   HT STANDS FOR 'HIT'.  (THE STUDENT 'HITS' THE ANSWER)
       IT IS 0 FOR INCORRECT AND 1 FOR CORRECT.
6020   HT = 0
6030   IF SA$ = A$ THEN HT = 1
6040   RETURN
7000   REM   KEEP SCORE
7010   REM   Q IS A COUNTER TO KEEP TRACK OF THE NUMBER OF QUESTIONS

7020   Q = Q + 1
7030   REM   SC IS A COUNTER (SCORE) TO KEEP TRACK OF NO. OF CORRECT
       ANSWERS.
7040   IF HT = 1 THEN SC = SC + 1
7050   RETURN
```

(continued)

```
8000   REM   PROVIDE FEEDBACK
8010   REM   FOR CORRECT ANSWERS
8020   IF HT = 1 THEN   GOSUB 9000
8030   REM   FOR INCORRECT ANSWERS
8040   IF HT = 0 THEN   GOSUB 10000
8050   RETURN
9000   REM   POSITIVE FEEDBACK
9010   PRINT "GREAT!"
9020   REM   PAUSE
9030 DE = 2000
9040   GOSUB 11000
9050   RETURN
10000   REM   NEGATIVE FEEDBACK
10010   HOME
10020   VTAB 10
10030   PRINT "SORRY!   THE ANSWER TO:"
10040   PRINT
10050   PRINT Q$
10060   PRINT
10070   PRINT "IS ";
10080   IF A$ = "T" THEN   PRINT "TRUE."
10090   IF A$ = "F" THEN   PRINT "FALSE."
10100   REM   PAUSE
10110 DE = 3000
10120   GOSUB 11000
10130   RETURN
11000   REM   DELAY LOOP
11010   FOR I = 1 TO DE
11020   NEXT I
11030   RETURN
12000   REM   PRESENT SCORE
12010   PRINT
12020   PRINT
12030   PRINT "YOU HAVE GOTTEN ";SC;" OUT OF ";Q
12040   PRINT "QUESTIONS CORRECT."
12050   PRINT
12060   REM   LAST BIT OF FEEDBACK -- CHECK PERCENTAGES
12070   IF SC / Q = < .5 THEN   PRINT "BETTER STUDY HARDER!"
12080   IF SC / Q > .5 AND SC / Q = < .75 THEN   PRINT "THAT IS PRE
       TTY GOOD!"
12090   IF SC / Q > .75 THEN   PRINT "VERY GOOD!"
12100   RETURN
13000   REM   RESERVED FOR LATER DEVELOPMENT
14000   REM   DATA
14010   DATA   "HYDROGEN IS THE LIGHTEST ELEMENT.","T"
14020   DATA   "HELIUM IS A HALOGEN GAS.","F"
14030   DATA   "SODIUM IS AN ACTIVE METAL.","T"
14040   DATA   "CHLORINE IS AN ACTIVE GAS.","T"
14050   DATA   "999","999"
```

```
******************************
*                            *
*      SCORE REPORTER        *
*                            *
*   -->TABLE OF VARIABLES<--  *
*                            *
******************************
```

A$ - ANSWER
3010 6030 10080 10090

(continued)

```
DE - DELAY VALUE
9030 10110 11010

HT - HIT
6020 6030 7040 8020 8040

I - COUNTER
11010 11020

Q - NUMBER OF QUESTIONS
7020 7020 12030 12070 12080 12080 12090

Q$ - QUESTION
180 3010 4040 10050

SA$ - STUDENT ANSWER
5010 5030 5030 6030

SC - SCORE
7040 7040 12030 12070 12080 12080 12090

END OF VAR. LIST
```

Disk Scorekeeper

When you want to keep track of individual scores for a long time, you must automatically store them on the computer disk. I do not recommend that you attempt scorekeeping on cassette tapes. This invariably fails, quite often with important programs being erased in the process. The following program is specific for the Apple II and will require modifications in the disk commands to make it work on other computers. Because disk-operating systems vary widely, I leave this to you. The process used here is clumsy, but it works well. The computer reads all the scores from the disk into its memory, then adds the most recent score to the bottom of the list. It then removes the old file from the disk and stores the new (and slightly longer) list in its place. As long as there is room on the disk, and the file does not become extremely large, this process works well. It is also the least complicated method.

```
*****************************
*                           *
*      DISK SCOREKEEPER     *
*                           *
*          ORWIG            *
*****************************
```

```
10  REM  A DISK STORAGE SCORING ROUTINE
20  REM  THE FOLLOWING LINE STORES 'CONTROL-D' IN D$.  THIS IS THE
         SYMBOL WHICH ACTIVATES THE DISK COMMANDS FOR APPLE II.
```

(continued)

```
30 D$ =  CHR$ (4)
100   REM   START OF MAIN PROGRAM
110   REM   INITIALIZE DISK FILE
120   GOSUB 1010
130   REM   GET NAME
140   GOSUB 2000
150   REM   GET QUESTION
160   GOSUB 3000
170   REM   CHECK FOR END OF QUESTIONS
180   IF Q$ = "999" THEN  GOTO 310
190   REM   SHOW QUESTION
200   GOSUB 4000
210   REM   ACCEPT ANSWER
220   GOSUB 5000
230   REM   JUDGE ANSWER
240   GOSUB 6000
250   REM   KEEP SCORE
260   GOSUB 7000
270   REM   PROVIDE FEEDBACK
280   GOSUB 8000
290   REM   GO BACK FOR ANOTHER QUESTION
300   GOTO 160
310   REM   PRESENT SCORE
320   GOSUB 12000
330   REM   STORE SCORE ON DISK
340   GOSUB 13000
350   REM   END OF MAIN PROGRAM
360   END
1000   REM   START OF ROUTINES
1010   REM   INITIALIZE DISK FILE
1020   PRINT D$;"OPEN SCORES"
1030   REM   STORE FILE IN A ARRAYS
1040   PRINT D$;"READ SCORES"
1050   INPUT N
1060   DIM NA$(N + 1),SC(N + 1)
1070   IF N = 0 THEN 1110
1080   FOR I = 1 TO N
1090   INPUT NA$(I),SC(I)
1100   NEXT I
1110   PRINT D$;"CLOSE SCORES"
1120   RETURN
2000   REM   GET NAME
2010   HOME
2020   VTAB 10
2030   PRINT "WHAT IS YOUR NAME?"
2040   INPUT NA$
2050   RETURN
3000   REM   GET QUESTION
3010   READ Q$,A$
3020   RETURN
4000   REM   SHOW THE QUESTION
4010   HOME
4020   PRINT "           TRUE OR FALSE?"
4030   VTAB 10
4040   PRINT Q$
4050   PRINT
4060   RETURN
5000   REM   GET STUDENT'S ANSWER
5010   GET SA$
5020   REM MAKE CERTAIN IT IS A 'T' OR AN 'F'
5030   IF SA$ <  > "T" AND SA$ <  > "F" THEN  GOTO 5010
```

(continued)

```
5040   RETURN
6000   REM   JUDGE ANSWER
6010   REM   HT STANDS FOR 'HIT'.  (THE STUDENT 'HITS' THE ANSWER)
       IT IS 0 FOR INCORRECT AND 1 FOR CORRECT.
6020 HT = 0
6030   IF SA$ = A$ THEN HT = 1
6040   RETURN
7000   REM   KEEP SCORE
7010   REM   Q IS A COUNTER TO KEEP TRACK OF THE NUMBER OF QUESTIONS

7020 Q = Q + 1
7030   REM   SC IS A COUNTER (SCORE) TO KEEP TRACK OF NO. OF CORRECT
       ANSWERS.
7040   IF HT = 1 THEN SC = SC + 1
7050   RETURN
8000   REM   PROVIDE FEEDBACK
8010   REM   FOR CORRECT ANSWERS
8020   IF HT = 1 THEN   GOSUB 9000
8030   REM   FOR INCORRECT ANSWERS
8040   IF HT = 0 THEN   GOSUB 10000
8050   RETURN
9000   REM   POSITIVE FEEDBACK
9010   PRINT "GREAT!"
9020   REM   PAUSE
9030 DE = 2000
9040   GOSUB 11000
9050   RETURN
10000   REM   NEGATIVE FEEDBACK
10010   HOME
10020   VTAB 10
10030   PRINT "SORRY!   THE ANSWER TO:"
10040   PRINT
10050   PRINT Q$
10060   PRINT
10070   PRINT "IS ";
10080   IF A$ = "T" THEN   PRINT "TRUE."
10090   IF A$ = "F" THEN   PRINT "FALSE."
10100   REM   PAUSE
10110 DE = 3000
10120   GOSUB 11000
10130   RETURN
11000   REM   DELAY LOOP
11010   FOR I = 1 TO DE
11020   NEXT I
11030   RETURN
12000   REM   PRESENT SCORE
12010   PRINT
12020   PRINT
12030   PRINT "YOU HAVE GOTTEN ";SC;" OUT OF ";Q
12040   PRINT "QUESTIONS CORRECT."
12050   PRINT
12060   REM   LAST BIT OF FEEDBACK -- CHECK PERCENTAGES
12070   IF SC / Q = < .5 THEN   PRINT "BETTER STUDY HARDER!"
12080   IF SC / Q > .5 AND SC / Q = < .75 THEN   PRINT "THAT IS PRE
        TTY GOOD!"
12090   IF SC / Q > .75 THEN   PRINT "VERY GOOD!"
12100   RETURN
13000   REM   STORE SCORES
13010   REM   STORE CURRENT NAME AND SCORE IN LAST PLACE IN ARRAYS
13020 NA$(N + 1) = NA$
13030 SC(N + 1) = SC
```

(continued)

```
13040   REM   CLEAN OUT OLD FILE
13050   PRINT D$;"DELETE SCORES"
13060   PRINT D$;"OPEN SCORES"
13070   REM   WRITE IN NEW FILE
13080   PRINT D$;"WRITE SCORES"
13090   PRINT N + 1
13100   FOR I = 1 TO N + 1
13110   PRINT NA$(I)
13120   PRINT SC(I)
13130   NEXT I
13140   PRINT D$;"CLOSE SCORES"
13150   RETURN
14000   REM   DATA
14010   DATA  "HYDROGEN IS THE LIGHTEST ELEMENT.","T"
14020   DATA  "HELIUM IS A HALOGEN GAS.","F"
14030   DATA  "SODIUM IS AN ACTIVE METAL.","T"
14040   DATA  "CHLORINE IS AN ACTIVE GAS.","T"
14050   DATA  "999","999"
```

```
*******************************
*                             *
*      DISK SCORE KEEPER      *
*                             *
*   -->TABLE OF VARIABLES<--  *
*                             *
*******************************
```

A$ - ANSWER
3010 6030 10080 10090

D$ - CONTROL D
30 1020 1040 1110 13050 13060 13080 13140

DE - DELAY VALUE
9030 10110 11010

HT - HIT
6020 6030 7040 8020 8040

I - COUNTER
1080 1090 1090 1100 11010 11020 13100 13110 13120 13130

N - NUMBER OF NAMES IN SCORES
1050 1060 1060 1070 1080 13020 13030 13090 13100

NA$ - NAME
2040 13020

NA$(*) - NAME ARRAY
1060 1090 13020 13110

Q - NUMBER OF QUESTIONS
7020 7020 12030 12070 12080 12080 12090

Q$ - QUESTION
180 3010 4040 10050

(continued)

```
SA$ - STUDENT ANSWER
5010 5030 5030 6030

SC - SCORE
7040 7040 12030 12070 12080 12080 12090 13030

SC(*) - SCORE ARRAY
1060 1090 13030 13120

END OF VAR. LIST
```

Score Reader

The following program, once again specific for the Apple II, allows a teacher to examine the file created by the previous program. It opens the file, checks its size, and then dimensions arrays accordingly. The computer then stores the contents of the file in those arrays. Following this, the computer prints out the arrays on the screen.

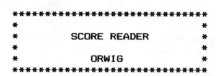

```
10  REM  FILE READING PROGRAM FOR APPLE II.
20  REM   THIS PROGRAM WILL READ NAMES AND SCORES FROM A DISK FILE,
          THEN IT WILL PRINT THEM OUT.
30  D$ =  CHR$ (4)
40   PRINT D$;"OPEN SCORES"
50   PRINT D$;"READ SCORES"
60   REM  GET THE SIZE OF FILE
70   INPUT N
80   IF N = 0 THEN 140
90   DIM NA$(N),SC(N)
100  REM  STORE DATA IN ARRAYS
110  FOR I = 1 TO N
120  INPUT NA$(I),SC(I)
130  NEXT I
140  PRINT D$;"CLOSE SCORES"
150  REM  PRINT NAMES AND SCORES
160  FOR I = 1 TO N
170  PRINT NA$(I),SC(I)
180  NEXT I
190  END
```

(continued)

```
*******************************
*                             *
*        SCORE READER         *
*                             *
*    -->TABLE OF VARIABLES<--  *
*                             *
*******************************
```

D$ - CONTROL D
30 40 50 140

I - COUNTER
110 120 120 130 160 170 170 180

N - SIZE OF FILE
70 80 90 90 110 160

NA$(*) - NAME ARRAY
90 120 170

SC(*) - SCORE ARRAY
90 120 170

END OF VAR. LIST

Set-Scores File

The following is a utility program used with the previous two programs. This program creates a clean scores file for use by the other two programs. It should be run to create the scores file and to clean it out when you are ready for a new batch of students. Once again, this program is specific to the Apple II.

```
*******************************
*                             *
*       SET-SCORES FILE       *
*                             *
*           ORWIG             *
*******************************
```

```
10  REM  A DISK FILE PROGRAM FOR APPLE II.
20  REM  THIS LITTLE PROGRAM SHOULD BE RUN TO CREATE THE 'SCORES'
        FILE.
30  REM  IT SHOULD ALSO BE USED TO CLEAR OUT ALL NAMES FROM AN OLD
        'SCORES' FILE.
40  REM  THE NEXT LINE STORES 'CONTROL-D' IN D$.  THIS IS THE SYMB
        OL USED BY APPLE IN DISK COMMANDS.
50  D$ =  CHR$ (4)
60  PRINT D$;"OPEN SCORES"
```

(continued)

```
70   PRINT D$;"DELETE SCORES"
80   PRINT D$;"OPEN SCORES"
90   PRINT D$;"WRITE SCORES"
100  REM  STORE THE VALUE'0' IN THE NEW SCORES FILE.
110  PRINT 0
120  PRINT D$;"CLOSE SCORES"
```

```
******************************
*                            *
*      SET-SCORES FILE        *
*                            *
*   -->TABLE OF VARIABLES<--  *
*                            *
******************************
```

```
D$ - CONTROL D
50 60 70 80 90 120

END OF VAR. LIST
```

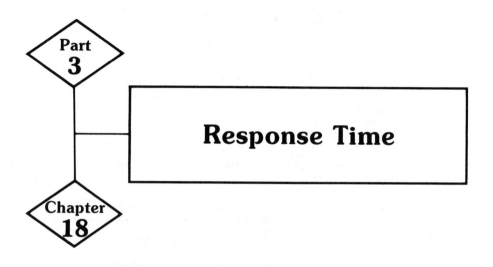

Response Time

Frequently in instructional computing it is necessary to time a student. The following routine establishes the basic technique to check the amount of time to press a key on the keyboard. This fundamental routine can be used for a variety of applications, ranging from reaction-time games to checks of fast or slow key responses in typing practice. The same technique will work on a variety of computers as long as you use the appropriate keyboard check and the appropriate accuracy adjustment. The accuracy adjustment is found most easily by trial and error.

```
***********************************
*                                 *
*          RESPONSE TIME          *
*                                 *
*             ORWIG               *
***********************************
```

```
10  REM   THIS IS AN APPLE PROGRAM DESIGNED TO TIME A RESPONSE.
20  REM   AD IS AN ACCURACY ADJUSTMENT WHICH WILL PROBABLY VARY FRO
      M APPLE TO APPLE.
50 AD = 68.8
100  REM   START OF MAIN PROGRAM
```

(continued)

```
110   REM  JUMP TO TIMER
120   GOSUB 1000
130   REM  PRINT RESULT
140   GOSUB 2000
150   REM  END OF MAIN PROGRAM
160   END
1000   REM  START OF ROUTINES
1010   HOME
1020   PRINT "TIMING!"
1030   PRINT "PRESS ANY KEY TO STOP"
1040   REM  TIMER
1050   IF  PEEK (49152) > 128 THEN 1080
1060 T = T + 1
1070   GOTO 1050
1080   POKE 49168,0
1090   RETURN
2000   REM  REPORT TIME
2010   PRINT  INT ((T / AD) * 10) / 10;" SECONDS"
2020   RETURN
```

```
*******************************
*                             *
*         RESPONSE TIME       *
*                             *
*    -->TABLE OF VARIABLES<--  *
*                             *
*******************************
```

AD - ACCURACY ADJUSTMENT
50 2010

T - TIME COUNT
1060 1060 2010

END OF VAR. LIST

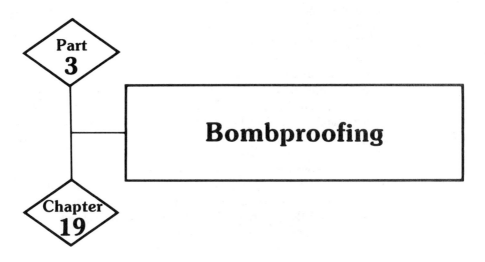

Part
3

Bombproofing

Chapter
19

The key to making a program run reliably is to anticipate all possible things that a person might do that he or she should not do. While there is little defense against a determined program wrecker, you should try to take steps to prevent a program from coming to a crashing halt (called a fatal error) when an uninformed learner accidentally presses the wrong button.

As you might guess, "nonfatal" errors don't make the program stop, but they prevent efficient use of the program. These errors most often occur when you program the computer to accept a certain answer, but the student responds with an acceptable alternative. The program doesn't recognize the alternative and promptly pronounces it incorrect. The result is usually instant antagonism. The following discussion and programs address both of these problem areas.

There are three "fatal" buttons that are extremely difficult to defend against. These are the On/Off Switch, the Reset key, and the Break key. While not all microcomputers have clearly defined Reset and Break keys, these functions can usually be created by some series of keystrokes. Probably the best protection against the unintentional use of these keys is to simply tell students that they will have to start the lesson all over if they should push one of these keys.

Beyond this, some computers allow limited protection against the pressing of the Reset and Break keys. This protection varies from one brand of computer to another in effectiveness and ease of application, so you will have to work through the specific manuals to determine what to do.

A more common problem is the fatal error which arises when an unexpected response is given to an INPUT or GET command. If a program asks a student to supply a number which is to be divided into other numbers, most computers will stumble when the student supplies the number 0. A simple solution is to check the number to see if it is zero before attempting any division.

A fatal error will also occur in many computers when the wrong type of value is supplied to the variable in the INPUT or GET commands. For example, pressing any letter key to supply a response to GET N on an Apple II will cause a fatal error. The simplest solution to this problem is to accept a string variable (GET N$), then use the VAL function to convert the string back to a digit if it is really needed.

The above are only a couple of examples of possible problem areas. Because of the wide diversity of reactions among microcomputers, there is no way to detail every possible fatal error. The best advice is to pay close attention to those parts of the program which accept information from the learner. Before you are convinced that your program will perform reliably, try every possible response you can think of. Not only should the program catch deadly input before it can cause a fatal error, but it should also provide feedback to the learner regarding the appropriate format for further input.

Multiple-Choice GET Command

The following program shows an acceptable technique for using the GET command for accepting answers to a multiple-choice question. Notice that the question can be answered by selecting A, B, C, or D and that a string variable has been used to store the selection. With this combination there is no way a normal key response can cause a fatal error. For other computers, the GET command will require slight modification.

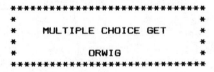

```
***********************************
*                                 *
*      MULTIPLE CHOICE GET        *
*                                 *
*             ORWIG               *
***********************************
```

```
10   REM   MULTIPLE CHOICE GET COMMAND
100  REM   START OF MAIN PROGRAM
110  HOME
120  PRINT : PRINT
130  PRINT "WHAT IS THE BEST WAY TO SNARFLE THE"
```

(continued)

```
140   PRINT "KIBENZEL OF A SNAZBERNG?"
150   PRINT
160   PRINT "     A. QUICKLY"
170   PRINT "     B. SLOWLY"
180   PRINT "     C. CAREFULLY"
190   PRINT "     D. NEVER"
200   PRINT
210   GET SA$
220   REM  IN CASE YOU DON'T KNOW, THE CORRECT ANSWER IS C!
230   REM  NOTE THAT ONLY A SINGLE LETTER CAN BE JUDGED
240   IF SA$ = "C" THEN 270
250   PRINT "SORRY, TRY AGAIN."
260   GOTO 210
270   PRINT "YOU ARE CORRECT!"
280   END
```

```
*******************************
*                             *
*     MULTIPLE CHOICE GET      *
*                             *
*   -->TABLE OF VARIABLES<--   *
*                             *
*******************************
```

```
SA$ - STUDENT RESPONSE
210 240

END OF VAR. LIST
```

Multiple Choice-Multiple Answer

While not usually the cause of fatal errors, there are times when a variety of answers might be acceptable. The following program demonstrates such a possibility with a multiple-choice question, but these situations are also found in fill-in-the-blank kinds of questions. The IF-OR-OR-THEN format can be extended to cover a variety of acceptable answers. If such an option is not allowed when it is really needed, students will rapidly become frustrated.

```
*********************************
*                               *
*   MULT. CHOICE - MULT. ANSWER  *
*                               *
*            ORWIG               *
*********************************
```

```
10   REM  MULTIPLE CHOICE - MULTIPLE ANSWERS
100  REM  START OF MAIN PROGRAM
```

(continued)

```
110   HOME
120   PRINT : PRINT
130   PRINT "WHAT IS THE BEST WAY TO SNARFLE THE"
140   PRINT "KIBENZEL OF A SNAZBERNG?"
150   PRINT
160   PRINT "     A. QUICKLY"
170   PRINT "     B. SLOWLY"
180   PRINT "     C. CAREFULLY"
190   PRINT "     D. NEVER"
200   PRINT
210   INPUT SA$
220   REM   IN CASE YOU DON'T KNOW, THE CORRECT ANSWER IS C!
230   REM   NOTE THE MULTIPLE JUDGEMENTS
240   IF SA$ = "C" OR SA$ = "C." OR SA$ = "CAREFULLY" THEN 270
250   PRINT "SORRY, TRY AGAIN."
260   GOTO 210
270   PRINT "YOU ARE CORRECT!"
280   END
```

```
********************************
*                              *
*MULT. CHOICE - MULT. ANSWER *
*                              *
*   -->TABLE OF VARIABLES<--   *
*                              *
********************************
```

```
SA$ - STUDENT RESPONSE
210 240 240 240

END OF VAR. LIST
```

Input Filter

As mentioned previously, there are times when input needs to be screened before any processing takes place. This procedure is usually referred to as "filtering," and an example follows. In this case, input is accepted into a string variable and checked to see if letters or digits are present. If letters are present, the student is told to use digits. If digits are present, they are transfered to a number variable and processing proceeds as normal. Over a period of time an instructional programmer can develop a wide variety of filters for a variety of purposes. The use of subroutines and "flags" (as explained in the listing) allows maximum flexibility in their use.

```
*******************************
*                             *
*        INPUT FILTER         *
*                             *
*           ORWIG             *
*******************************
```

```
10   REM   INPUT FILTER
100  REM   START OF MAIN PROGRAM
110  REM   GET SOME NUMBERS
120  GOSUB 1000
130  REM   PRINT A QUESTION
140  HOME
150  PRINT "WHAT IS THE PRODUCT OF ";N1;" AND ";N2;"?"
160  REM   INPUT AN ANSWER INTO A STRING VARIABLE
170  INPUT SA$
180  REM   GO FILTER THE ANSWER
190  GOSUB 2000
200  REM   CHECK FOR PROPER FORM
210  IF F = 0 THEN 260
220  PRINT "SORRY, I CAN'T UNDERSTAND YOUR ANSWER."
230  PRINT "USE NUMBERS LIKE 10, NOT WORDS LIKE TEN."
240  F = 0
250  GOTO 150
260  REM   CHECK FOR PROPER ANSWER
270  IF SA = N1 * N2 THEN 300
280  PRINT "SORRY, THAT IS NOT CORRECT.   TRY AGAIN."
290  GOTO 150
300  PRINT "CORRECT!"
310  PRINT "WOULD YOU LIKE ANOTHER PROBLEM?
320  INPUT SA$
330  IF  LEFT$ (SA$,1) = "Y" THEN 100
340  PRINT "GOODBYE FOR NOW!"
350  END
1000  REM   RANDOMIZING
1010 N1 =   INT ( RND (1) * 15)
1020 N2 =   INT ( RND (1) * 15)
1030  RETURN
2000  REM   FILTER INPUT
2010  REM CHECK FOR A "0" ANSWER
2020  IF SA$ = "0" THEN 2070
2030  REM   IF "VAL" RETURNS A 0 THEN LETTERS WERE USED
2040  REM   IN THAT CASE, SET THE FLAG "F" TO 1
2050  IF  VAL (SA$) = 0 THEN F = 1
2060  REM   SET A NUMBER VARIABLE TO THE "VALUE" OF THE STRING
2070 SA =   VAL (SA$)
2080  RETURN
```

```
*******************************
*                             *
*        INPUT FILTER         *
*                             *
*   -->TABLE OF VARIABLES<--  *
*                             *
*******************************
```

F - FLAG
210 240 2050

(continued)

```
N1 - ONE RANDOM NUMBER
150 270 1010

N2 - ANOTHER RANDOM NO.
150 270 1020

SA - STUDENT ANSWER - NO.
270 2070

SA$ - STUDENT ANSWER - STRING
170 320 330 2020 2050 2070

END OF VAR. LIST
```

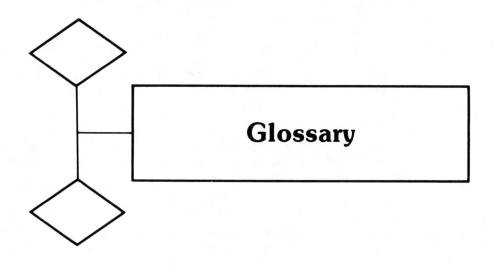

Glossary

ADDRESS

A number that designates a location where information is stored in a memory device.

AFFECTIVE DOMAIN

The area of human learning that deals with feelings, attitudes, and beliefs.

ALGORITHM

A statement of mathematical or logical steps to be followed in the solution of a problem.

ARRAY

A technique for storing and manipulating information in the computer's memory. It is smilar in concept to a list or chart on paper.

ASCII

American Standard Code for Information Interchange. A standard set of binary codes that represent letters, numbers, and symbols.

ASSEMBLER

A program that converts an assembly language (usually English mnemonics) into a machine language.

ASSEMBLY LANGUAGE

A computer language that uses shorthand forms to represent one or more machine-language instructions.

BASIC

Beginners All-Purpose Symbolic Instruction Code. A high-level conversational programming language in wide use. Incorporates simple English words and common mathematical symbols.

BASIC-IN-ROM

The BASIC language has been stored in *Read Only Memory.* In this case the language "resides" in the computer and can't be accidentally erased.

BATCH PROCESSING

A technique of submitting programs to a computer in bunches. The computer processes programs one after the other with no provision for intermediate user input. Efficient use of computer time. Contrasts with *interactive processing.*

BAUD

A rate of data transfer given in bits per second. Alphabetic characters usually require about 10 bits per character; a baud rate of 300 corresponds to about 30 characters per second.

BINARY CODE

The most fundamental of codes, using only ones and zeros to represent data. Can be represented by the presence or absence of electrical current within key parts of a computer.

BIT

A single binary digit, represented by a zero or a one. It takes several bits combined to make any meaningful code. Quite often eight bits are put togethor to make a byte.

BOOLEAN ALGEBRA

A system of logic design that was invented by George Boole. Utilizes simple functions such as AND, OR, NOT, NOR, etc.

BRANCHING INSTRUCTION

Individualized instruction that adjusts to the capabilities of each learner by taking various branches through the content.

BUG

Something that prevents a program from working properly. Usually an error in typing or program design, although sometimes a malfunction within the computer itself.

BUS

The set of electrical lines connecting the various parts of the computer. Data and control signals are sent along these lines.

BYTE

A basic unit of information in a computer. A byte usually represents one character and is normally eight bits in length.

CAI

Computer-*assisted* *i*nstruction. Any instruction that utilizes the computer as the primary vehicle for delivery.

CHARACTER

Letters, numbers, and symbols that can be arranged into information. A character can usually be defined with one byte of data.

CHARACTER SET

Those characters available to any one particular computer or peripheral device. Some devices have a limited character set; for example, some printers can print only capital letters.

CLOCK

The internal pace-setter of a computer. The clock keeps a number of events within the computer working together at an even pace.

COGNITIVE DOMAIN

The area of human learning that involves thinking, reasoning, and problem-solving activities.

COMPILER

A program that translates a high-level language into a machine-readable program. Normally allows the computer to execute a program much more rapidly.

COMPUTERESE

A slang term that represents the new terminology associated with computers. The terminology is almost like a foreign language.

COURSE-WRITING SYSTEM

A highly specialized program designed to allow novices to create CAI with a minimum of trouble.

CPU

Central *processing unit.* The "brain" of the computer. Directs all the functions of the computer.

CRASH

The sudden appearance of some defect in hardware or software that causes the computer to come to a screeching halt.

CRT

Cathode *ray tube.* The tube that makes the television screen. Used to display text and graphics created by a computer. Frequently linked with a keyboard to create a CRT terminal.

CURSOR

A movable spot on the face of a CRT that indicates where the next character will be displayed.

DATA

Information transferred to or from a computer.

DEBUG

The process of locating and eliminating errors.

DESCENDER

The bottom part of such letters as *p*, *y*, and *j*. If they descend below the line of print, they are called descenders. Descenders are desirable because they make text easier to read.

DIAGNOSTIC ROUTINE

A form of program that lets the computer test itself for internal hardware malfunctions.

DISC (DISK)

A mass storage device capable of high storage and retrieval speeds. Similar in appearance to a magnetic oxide-coated record. Can be either *floppy* or *hard*, depending on performance requirements.

DISTRACTOR

A distractor is a wrong answer in a multiple-choice selection. The closer the distractors resemble the correct answer, the harder the question becomes.

DOS

Disc-operating system. A collection of programs that combine with an interface to allow a computer to control a disc machine.

DOT MATRIX

A technique of using an array of dots to create characters. A standard five-by-seven array of dots is the minimum for alphabetic characters, while larger arrays, such as seven-by-nine, will allow letters with descenders and under-lining.

DRILL AND PRACTICE

A repetitive process used to refine an emerging skill or concept. It is usually used in conjunction with other teaching technique.

DUPLEX (FULL DUPLEX)

An interface that allows simultaneous two-way communication between a computer and a peripheral device.

EGRULE

In CAI, this is a technique of providing examples before the rule that explains the examples is stated. Contrasts with RULEG.

ENABLING OBJECTIVE

One or more subobjectives required before a terminal objective can be achieved.

ENTRY SKILLS

Those skills that a learner posses when he or she enters a unit of instruction. See *tool skills*.

EPROM

*E*rasable *p*rogrammable *r*ead *o*nly *m*emory. A long-term memory that under special conditions can be rewritten.

EXECUTION

The actual running of a program.

EXTERNAL STORAGE (MASS MEMORY)

Data storage through a peripheral device such as a tape or disk.

FEEDBACK

Information that the learner receives from the computer during CAI. It may be either positive or negative, immediate or delayed.

FILE

A set of data that have some specified relationship.

FIRMWARE

Programs that are stored in ROM. They are immediately available for execution; there is no need to load them from a storage device.

FLOPPY DISC(K)

A semiflexible (but don't bend it) magnetic medium used for storing programs and data. Popular with CAI developers because of its ease of use.

FLOWCHART

A graphic technique used to map the flow of a program before it is actually developed.

FORTRAN

*For*mula *tran*slator. A high-level language oriented toward math and science applications.

FRAME

In CAI applications this is a single screenful of information.

GIGO

*G*arbage *i*n, *g*arbage *o*ut. Any errors that enter a computer will result in errors in the output.

GOAL

What the instructor wants the learners to gain from the instruction.

GRAPHICS

The ability of a computer to construct line drawings, graphs, charts, etc., on a CRT or printer.

HALF DUPLEX

An interface that allows either reception or transmission of data but *does not* allow both to occur simultaneously.

HARDCOPY

Computer output that is printed onto paper. Contrasts with the temporary image presented on a CRT.

HARDWARE

The equipment that makes up a computer system.

HEXADECIMAL SYSTEM

A number system based on 16. Uses the digits 0-9 and the letters A-F.

HIGH-LEVEL LANGUAGE

A computer language with characteristics of English words, decimal arithmetic, and common mathematical symbols. Each instruction usually represents many individual computer operations.

IC

Integrated circuit. Miniaturized electronic devices that have many distinct components integrated into self-contained circuits. Responsible for the reduction of room-sized computers into desk-top units.

INPUT

Information (or data) entering a computer or peripheral device. The same information may be *output* from some other part of the system.

INTERACTIVE

A computer and program that maintain communication with the user during operation. Allows the use of the computer for instruction.

INTERFACE

A hardware or software device used to connect a computer to peripheral equipment.

INTERPRETER

A program that translates a language (usually into machine code) as it is being executed.

I/O

Input/output of information. The two terms are frequently used together because they often involve the same communication lines.

K (KILO)

Symbol or prefix for 1,000. In computer language, 1 K actually stands for 2 to the 10th power, or 1,024.

LANGUAGE

The method by which one communicates with a computer. Languages vary from machine-level codes through high-level types, such as BASIC.

LINEAR INSTRUCTION

CAI in which all learners proceed through the same instruction. No allowance is made for individual differences.

LOAD

The process of inserting information (a program or data) into a computer.

MACHINE LANGUAGE

A language that can be executed directly by the computer. Usually a series of binary or hexadecimal numbers. Difficult for humans to use.

MASS STORAGE

Devices such as disks or tapes that can store large quantities of programs and data. These programs and data must be loaded into the computer's RAM before they can be used.

MEDIA ATTRIBUTE

Some characteristic of a particular form of medium that is a selling point. For example, the capability of immediate feedback is an attribute of CAI.

MEMORY

The high-speed electronic components in a computer that store information. Often called RAM and ROM.

MICROCOMPUTER

A small computer, usually desk-top in size. Microcomputers can process only 8 or 16 bits of information in any one step.

MNEMONIC

Intended to assist human memory. Usually abbreviations or related alphabetic characters. Examples are dvd for divide, sub for subtract, etc.

MODEM

*M*odulator-*de*modulator. An interface that allows computers to communicate over telephone lines.

MONITOR

A video display that allows the computer signal to enter the video circuitry directly. Contrasts with receiver.

MONOCHROME

A one-color video display. While this usually refers to black and white, black and green or black and orange is also common.

MOTHER BOARD

The circuit board in the microcomputer that interconnects the CPU with all other memory and support devices.

OBJECTIVE

A desired aspect of the instruction stated in a manner so that it can be measured.

OUTPUT

Information or data coming from a computer.

PARALLEL COMMUNICATION

A technique for the I/O of information that allows bytes (eight bits) to be transmitted simultaneously. Fast.

PASCAL

A relatively new high-level language. Named in honor of the French mathematician.

PEEK

A BASIC command that allows direct examination of memory.

PERIPHERAL DEVICE

Equipment that links to a computer. Printers, CRTs, and tape and disc drives are examples.

PILOT

A specialized language (called a *course-writing language*) that is good for creating instruction.

POKE

A BASIC command that allows information to be stored directly in memory.

PROGRAM

A series of instructions to a computer.

PROM

Programmable read only memory. Permanently recorded data stored on special RAM memory ICs. Once programmed, they can't be altered by computer or man. Useful for storing frequently utilized instructions.

PSYCHOMOTOR DOMAIN

The area of human learning that involves mind-muscle coordination. An example might be learning to work a video arcade game.

RAM

Random access memory. The "working" memory of the computer. This memory can be accessed and altered by the computer as needed. This form of memory is susceptible to power interruptions or program "bugs."

REAL TIME

If a computer simulation operates at the same pace as the real process, the simulation is said to take place in real time. Computer simulations can also proceed faster or slower than the real process normally would. Thus the life cycle of a lake can be depicted in a reasonable amount of time.

RECEIVER

A receiver is a standard television. It is designed to receive television signals from the air; in some cases it may not be good enough to present sharp computer images.

ROM

Read only memory. About the same as PROM, except that ROM is usually programmed at the time of manufacture. Can also refer to read only memories in general. Can't be altered by the computer or man.

RS232C

A standard of voltage levels used for the serial input/output of data. Commonly called RS-232.

RULEG

Stands for *rule before examples*. This is a technique frequently used in CAI. Contrasts with EGRULE.

RUN

A command used in may languages to start the execution of a program.

SERIAL TRANSMISSION

A technique of transmitting data over a communication line one bit at a time.

SIMULATION

A process of using the computer to model a process that can't be readily experienced in real life.

SOFTWARE

Programs and necessary documentation that are needed to make a computer "do its thing."

SPECIAL LANGUAGE

A language that is designed to do only one thing well. Pilot is an example of a special language; it is used to create instruction and can't be used for much of anything else.

STEP SIZE

The amount of new information presented in each frame of CAI.

STORYBOARD

A paper-and-pencil rendition of each frame of a CAI lesson. It can be used to test an idea before extensive program writing takes place.

STRING

A group of letters or symbols to be used by the computer. The student's name, answers to questions, and spelling words are examples of common strings.

TASK DESCRIPTION

A blow-by-blow account of every step required to accomplish a particular task.

TERMINAL

A peripheral device that usually consists of a printer or a CRT and a keyboard.

TERMINAL OBJECTIVE

The final objective required to demonstrate attainment of some concept or skill. Often requires attainment of several enabling objectives first.

TOOL SKILLS

Those skills or concepts required at the start of any particular CAI lesson.

TRANSPARENCY

The ability of a computer and its software to keep out of the way of the instruction. The computer should not become a distraction.

VOLATILE MEMORY

Any memory that does not retain its information when electrical power is lost.

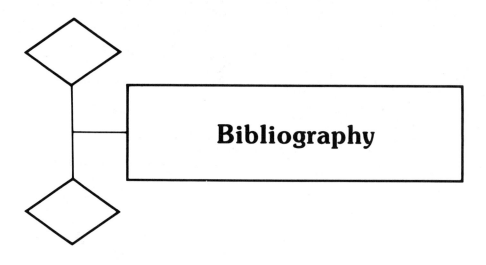

Bibliography

Boocock, Sarane, S. *Simulation Games in Learning*. Beverly Hills, Calif.: Sage Publications, 1968.

Brown, James W.; Lewis, Richard B.; and Harcleroad, Fred F. *AV Instruction: Technology, Media, and Methods*. New York: McGraw-Hill, 1977.

Bycer, Bernard, B. *Flowcharting: Programming, Software Designing, and Computer Problem Solving*. New York: Wiley, 1975.

Dahl, O. J.; Dijkstra, E. W.; and Hoare, C. A. R. *Structured Programming*. New York: Academic Press, 1972.

Davies, Ivor K. *Objectives in Curriculum Design*. New York: McGraw-Hill, 1976.

Davis, Robert H.; Alexander, Lawrence T.; and Yelon, Stephen L. *Learning System Design: An Approach to the Improvement of Instruction*. New York: McGraw-Hill, 1974.

Espich, James E., and Williams, Bill. *Developing Programmed Instruction Materials: A Handbook for Program Writers*. Palo Alto, Calif: Fearon Pub., 1967.

Farina, Mario V. *Flowcharting*. Englewood Cliffs, N.J.: Prentice-Hall, 1970.

Gagne, Robert M. *The Conditions of Learning*. New York: Holt, Rinehart, and Winston, 1970.

Gagne, Robert M., and Briggs, Leslie J. *Principles of Instructional Design*. New York: Holt, Rinehart, and Winston, 1974.

Graham, Neill. *The Mind Tool: Computers and Their Impact on Society*. New York: West Publishing, 1976.

Green, Edward J. *Learning Processes and Programmed Instruction*. New York: Holt, Rinehart, and Winston, 1962.

Gronlund, Norman E. *Individualizing Classroom Instruction*. New York: Macmillan, 1974.

Kemp, Jerrold E. *Planning and Producing Audiovisual Materials*. New York: T. Y. Crowell, 1975.

Kemp, Jerrold E. *Instructional Design: A Plan for Unit and Course Development*. Belmont, Calif.: Fearon Pub., 1977.

Langdon, Danny G. *Interactive Instructional Designs for Individualized Learning*. Englewood Cliffs, N.J.: Educational Technology Pub., 1973.

Lippy, Gerald. *Computer Assisted Test Construction*. Englewood Cliffs, N.J.: Educational Technology Pub., 1974.

Mager, Robert F. *Preparing Instructional Objectives*. Belmont, Calif.: Fearon Pub., 1975.

Orwig, Gary W., and Hodges, William S. *The Computer Tutor*. Cambridge: Winthrop Pub., 1982.

Popham, W. James. *Criterion Referenced Measurement*. Englewood Cliffs, N.J.: Educational Technology Pub, 1971.

Schriber, Thomas J. *Fundamentals of Flowcharting*. New York: Wiley, 1969.

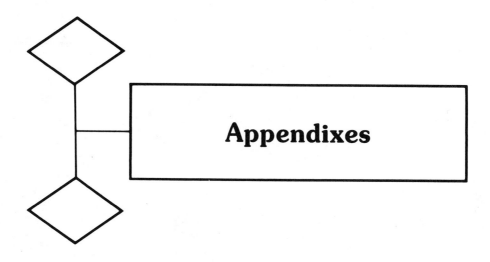

Appendixes

The appendixes in this section show sample programs that were referred to in Chapter 3. Appendix A shows a sample of a drill-and-practice program. Appendix B shows a sample linear program. Appendix C shows a sample branching program. Appendix D shows a sample simulation program.

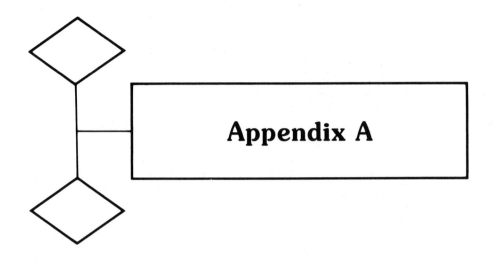

Appendix A

```
************************
*                      *
*        DRILL         *
*                      *
*        ORWIG         *
************************
```

```
10   REM   SAMPLE MULTIPLICATION DRILL BY GARY ORWIG
1000   REM   INTRODUCTION
1010 L = 24
1020   GOSUB 8000
1030   PRINT
1040   PRINT "**************************************"
1050   PRINT
1060   PRINT "        MULTIPLICATION DRILL"
1070   PRINT
1080   PRINT "**************************************"
1090 L = 10
1100   REM   SCROLL
1110   GOSUB 8000
1120 DE = 2000
1130   REM   DELAY
1140   GOSUB 9000
1150   REM   GET NAME
1160   PRINT "WHAT IS YOUR NAME";
1170   INPUT NA$
1180   PRINT
1190   PRINT
```

(continued)

```
1200   PRINT "I AM HAPPY TO MEET YOU, ";NA$;"."
1210   PRINT "WE ARE GOING TO PRACTICE SOME"
1220   PRINT "MULTIPLICATION PROBLEMS."
1230   REM   OPERATING PARAMETERS
1240   PRINT
1250   PRINT
1260   PRINT
1270   PRINT "HOW MANY PROBLEMS DO YOU"
1280   PRINT "WANT, ";NA$;
1290   INPUT NU
1300   PRINT
1310   PRINT "VERY GOOD, ";NU;" IT WILL BE!"
1320   PRINT
1330   PRINT "WHAT IS THE LARGEST NUMBER"
1340   PRINT "YOU WANT TO WORK WITH ";NA$;
1350   INPUT MX
1360   PRINT
1370   PRINT "GREAT!   I WILL TRY NOT TO GIVE YOU"
1380   PRINT "ANY NUMBERS OVER ";MX;"."
1390   PRINT
1400   PRINT "I AM NOW READY TO START!"
1410   PRINT
1420   REM   DELAY
1430 DE = 500
1440   GOSUB 9000
1450   PRINT "HERE WE GO!!"
1460   REM   DELAY
1470 DE = 500
1480   GOSUB 9000
1490   REM   SCROLL
1500 L = 4
1510   GOSUB 8000
2000   REM   MAIN PROGRAM
2010   REM   GET RANDOM NUMBERS
2020   GOSUB 3000
2030 HT = 1
2040 C = A * B
2050   PRINT
2060   PRINT
2070   PRINT A;" TIMES ";B;" EQUALS";
2080   INPUT SA
2090   REM   GO JUDGE ANSWER
2100   GOSUB 4000
2110   REM   PROVIDE FEEDBACK
2120   GOSUB 5000
2130   REM   KEEP SCORE
2140   GOSUB 7000
2150   REM   GET NEXT PROBLEM
2160   GOTO 2010
3000   REM   RANDOMIZING
3010 A =   INT (MX *   RND (1)) + 1
3020 B =   INT (MX *   RND (1)) + 1
3030   RETURN
4000   REM   JUDGE ANSWER
4010   IF SA = C THEN 4070
4020   GOSUB 6000
4030   PRINT
4040   PRINT "TRY AGAIN!"
4050   INPUT SA
4060   GOTO 4010
```

(continued)

```
4070    RETURN
5000    REM  REWARDS
5010    PRINT
5020  I =   INT (5 *  RND (1)) + 1
5030    ON I GOTO 5050,5070,5090,5110,5130
5040    REM  REWARDS
5050    PRINT "GREAT!"
5060    RETURN
5070    PRINT "SUPER!"
5080    RETURN
5090    PRINT "FANTASTIC!"
5100    RETURN
5110    PRINT "YOU'RE REALLY GOING NOW, ";NA$
5120    RETURN
5130    PRINT "THAT'S GREAT, ";NA$
5140    RETURN
6000    REM  WRONG ANSWER
6010    PRINT
6020    IF HT = 0 THEN 6050
6030  WR = WR + 1
6040  HT = 0
6050  I =   INT (5 *  RND (1)) + 1
6060    ON I GOTO 6080,6100,6120,6140,6160
6070    REM  WRONGS
6080    PRINT "OOPS!"
6090    RETURN
6100    PRINT "LOOK CLOSER, ";NA$
6110    RETURN
6120    PRINT "NO...."
6130    RETURN
6140    PRINT "ARE YOU PAYING ATTENTION, ";NA$
6150    RETURN
6160    PRINT "SORRY!"
6170    RETURN
7000    REM  SCORE KEEPING
7010  TL = TL + 1
7020    IF TL = NU THEN 10000
7030    RETURN
8000    REM  SCROLLING
8010    FOR I = 1 TO L
8020    PRINT
8030    NEXT I
8040    RETURN
9000    REM  DELAY
9010    FOR I = 1 TO DE
9020    NEXT I
9030    RETURN
10000    REM  CLOSING
10010    PRINT
10020    PRINT "THAT'S ALL!"
10030    PRINT
10040    PRINT "I HOPE YOU HAD FUN, ";NA$
10050    PRINT
10060    PRINT
10070    PRINT
10080    PRINT "YOU HAD ";NU - WR;" OUT OF "
10090    PRINT NU;" PROBLEMS CORRECT!"
10100    END
```

```
******************************
*                            *
*            DRILL           *
*                            *
*    -->TABLE OF VARIABLES<-- *
*                            *
******************************
```

A - ONE NUMBER
2040 2070 3010

B - OTHER NUMBER
2040 2070 3020

C - CORRECT ANSWER
2040 4010

DE - DELAY VALUE
1120 1430 1470 9010

HT - 'HIT' MARKER
2030 6020 6040

I - COUNTER
5020 5030 6050 6060 8010 8030 9010 9020

L - LINES OF SCROLLING
1010 1090 1500 8010

MX - MAXIMUM VALUE
1350 1380 3010 3020

NA$ - NAME
1170 1200 1280 1340 5110 5130 6100 6140 10040

NU - NO. OF PROBLEMS
1290 1310 7020 10080 10090

SA - STUDENT'S ANSWER
2080 4010 4050

TL - TOTAL PROBLEMS GIVEN
7010 7010 7020

WR - NO. WRONG
6030 6030 10080

END OF VAR. LIST

```
]
]RUN


*******************************************

             MULTIPLICATION DRILL

*******************************************.

WHAT IS YOUR NAME?GARY


I AM HAPPY TO MEET YOU, GARY.
WE ARE GOING TO PRACTICE SOME
MULTIPLICATION PROBLEMS.


HOW MANY PROBLEMS DO YOU
WANT, GARY?5

VERY GOOD, 5 IT WILL BE!

WHAT IS THE LARGEST NUMBER
YOU WANT TO WORK WITH GARY?12

GREAT!   I WILL TRY NOT TO GIVE YOU
ANY NUMBERS OVER 12.

I AM NOW READY TO START!

HERE WE GO!!


6 TIMES 9 EQUALS?45

LOOK CLOSER, GARY

TRY AGAIN!
?54

SUPER!

9 TIMES 1 EQUALS?9

FANTASTIC!


4 TIMES 9 EQUALS?36

YOU'RE REALLY GOING NOW, GARY


8 TIMES 2 EQUALS?16

YOU'RE REALLY GOING NOW, GARY
```

(continued)

```
9 TIMES 4 EQUALS?35

OOPS!

TRY AGAIN!
?36

SUPER!

THAT'S ALL!

I HOPE YOU HAD FUN, GARY


YOU HAD 3 OUT OF
5 PROBLEMS CORRECT!
```

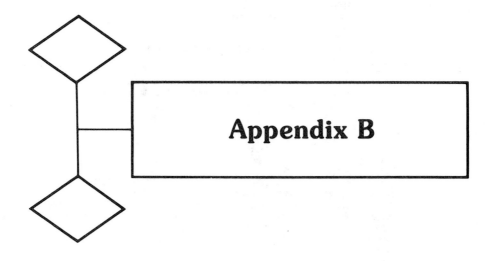

Appendix B

```
******************************
*                            *
*          LINEAR            *
*                            *
*          ORWIG             *
******************************
```

```
10   REM  A SAMPLE LINEAR PROGRAM BY GARY ORWIG
1000   REM   INTRODUCTION
1010 L = 24
1020   GOSUB 14000
1030   PRINT "          THE METRIC SYSTEM"
1040 L = 12
1050   GOSUB 14000
1060 DE = 1500
1070   GOSUB 15000
1080   PRINT "WHAT IS YOUR NAME?"
1090   INPUT NA$
1100 L = 24
1110   GOSUB 14000
1120   PRINT "I AM HAPPY TO MEET YOU, ";NA$;"."
1130   PRINT
1140   PRINT
1150   PRINT "IN THIS LESSON WE WILL BE STUDYING"
1160   PRINT "THE METRIC SYSTEM."
1170   PRINT
1180   PRINT "WE WILL LOOK AT THE BASIC UNITS OF"
1190   PRINT "MEASUREMENT FOR LENGTH, VOLUME, AND
```

(continued)

```
1200   PRINT "MASS.
1210 L = 10
1220   GOSUB 14000
1230   GOSUB 16000
2000   REM   TERM METRIC INTRO
2010 L = 24
2020   GOSUB 14000
2030   PRINT "LET'S BEGIN WITH THE TERM 'METRIC.'"
2040   PRINT
2050   PRINT
2060   PRINT "THE 'METRIC' SYSTEM GETS ITS NAME"
2070   PRINT "FROM ITS BASIC UNIT OF LENGTH, THE"
2080   PRINT "METER."
2090 L = 16
2100   GOSUB 14000
2110   GOSUB 16000
3000   REM   NAMED AFTER METER
3010 L = 24
3020   GOSUB 14000
3030   PRINT "THE METRIC SYSTEM WAS NAMED AFTER ITS"
3040   PRINT "BASIC UNIT OF LENGTH, WHICH IS "
3050   PRINT "THE ....."
3060 L = 16
3070   GOSUB 14000
3080   GOSUB 17000
3090 A$ = "METER"
3100   GOSUB 18000
3110   IF HT = 0 THEN 3000
4000   REM   LENGTH
4010 L = 24
4020   GOSUB 14000
4030   PRINT "THE METER IS THE METRIC SYSTEM'S"
4040   PRINT "BASIC UNIT OF ......."
4050 L = 16
4060   GOSUB 14000
4070   GOSUB 17000
4080 A$ = "LENGTH"
4090   GOSUB 18000
4100   IF HT = 0 THEN 4000
5000   REM   VOLUME INTRO
5010 L = 24
5020   GOSUB 14000
5030   PRINT "THE BASIC UNIT OF VOLUME IN THE METRIC"
5040   PRINT "SYSTEM IS THE 'LITER.'"
5050   PRINT
5060   PRINT "THE LITER IS USED TO MEASURE LIQUIDS"
5070   PRINT "AND GASES."
5080 L = 15
5090   GOSUB 14000
5100   GOSUB 16000
6000   REM   LITER
6010 L = 24
6020   GOSUB 14000
6030   PRINT "THE BASIC UNIT FOR MEASURING VOLUMES"
6040   PRINT "IN THE METRIC SYSTEM IS THE ......"
6050 L = 16
6060   GOSUB 14000
6070   GOSUB 17000
6080 A$ = "LITER"
6090   GOSUB 18000
6100   IF HT = 0 THEN 6000
7000   REM   LIQUIDS
```

(continued)

```
7010 L = 24
7020  GOSUB 14000
7030  PRINT "THE LITER IS USUALLY USED TO MEASURE"
7040  PRINT "GASES AND ........"
7050 L = 16
7060  GOSUB 14000
7070  GOSUB 17000
7080 A$ = "LIQUIDS"
7090  GOSUB 18000
7100  IF HT = 0 THEN 7000
8000  REM  MASS INTRO
8010 L = 24
8020  GOSUB 14000
8030  PRINT "IN THE METRIC SYSTEM, THE MEASUREMENT"
8040  PRINT "OF WEIGHT IS BASED ON MASS, THE AMOUNT"
8050  PRINT "OF MATTER AN OBJECT CONTAINS."
8060  PRINT
8070  PRINT "THE METRIC UNIT OF MASS IS THE 'GRAM.'"
8080  PRINT
8090  PRINT "THE GRAM IS USUALLY USED TO MEASURE"
8100  PRINT "SOLID THINGS."
8110 L = 12
8120  GOSUB 14000
8130  GOSUB 16000
9000  REM  MASS
9010 L = 24
9020  GOSUB 14000
9030  PRINT "THE METRIC SYSTEM BASES THE MEASUREMENT"
9040  PRINT "OF WEIGHT ON THE AMOUNT OF MATTER"
9050  PRINT "AN OBJECT CONTAINS."
9060  PRINT
9070  PRINT "THIS IS CALLED ....."
9080 L = 18
9090  GOSUB 14000
9100  GOSUB 17000
9110 A$ = "MASS"
9120  GOSUB 18000
9130  IF HT = 0 THEN 9000
10000  REM  GRAM
10010 L = 24
10020  GOSUB 14000
10030  PRINT "THE METRIC UNIT FOR MEASURING MASS"
10040  PRINT "IS CALLED THE ....."
10050 L = 20
10060  GOSUB 14000
10070  GOSUB 17000
10080 A$ = "GRAM"
10090  GOSUB 18000
10100  IF HT = 0 THEN 10000
11000  REM  SOLID THINGS
11010 L = 24
11020  GOSUB 14000
11030  PRINT "THE GRAM IS USUALLY USED TO MEASURE"
11040  PRINT "THINGS WHICH ARE ......"
11050 L = 20
11060  GOSUB 14000
11070  GOSUB 17000
11080 A$ = "SOLID"
11090  GOSUB 18000
11100  IF HT = 0 THEN 11000
12000  REM  FINISHED
12010 L = 24
```

(continued)

```
12020   GOSUB 14000
12030   PRINT "WE ARE FINISHED, ";NA$;"!"
12040 L = 12
12050   GOSUB 14000
12060   END
13000   REM    START OF SUBROUTINES
14000   REM    SCROLLING
14010   FOR I = 1 TO L
14020   PRINT
14030   NEXT I
14040   RETURN
15000   REM   DELAY
15010   FOR I = 1 TO DE
15020   NEXT I
15030   RETURN
16000   REM   KEY PROMPT
16010   REM   CHECK WITH NO SCROLLING
16020   VTAB 23
16030   PRINT "PRESS ANY KEY TO CONTINUE"
16040   FOR I = 1 TO 350
16050   IF   PEEK (49152) <  = 128 THEN 16080
16060   POKE 49168,0
16070   RETURN
16080   NEXT I
16090   REM   CHECK WITH SCROLLING
16100   IF   PEEK (49152) <  = 128 THEN 16130
16110   POKE 49168,0
16120   RETURN
16130   REM    ASSIGN MESSAGE TO B$
16140 B$ = "PRESS ANY KEY TO CONTINUE"
16150   GOSUB 16190
16160 B$ = "                         "
16170   GOSUB 16190
16180   GOTO 16090
16190   REM   SCROLLING ROUTINE
16200 BL =   LEN (B$)
16210   VTAB 23
16220   FOR I = 1 TO BL
16230   PRINT  MID$ (B$,I,1);
16240   FOR J = 1 TO 20: NEXT J
16250   NEXT I
16260   PRINT
16270   RETURN
17000   REM   GET STUDENT ANSWER
17010   VTAB 20
17020   PRINT "TYPE IN THE ANSWER HERE, THEN PRESS"
17030   PRINT "THE RETURN KEY."
17040   INPUT SA$
17050   RETURN
18000   REM   JUDGE ANSWER
18010 HT = 0
18020   IF SA$ = A$ THEN HT = 1
18030   IF HT = 0 THEN   GOSUB 19000
18040   IF HT = 1 THEN   GOSUB 20000
18050   RETURN
19000   REM   WRONG ANSWER
19010   FOR K = 1 TO 3
19020 B$ = "THE CORRECT ANSWER IS   " + A$ + " ."
19030   GOSUB 16190
19040 B$ = "                         "
19050   GOSUB 16190
19060   NEXT K
```

(continued)

```
19070   RETURN
20000   REM   CORRECT ANSWER
20010 L = 24
20020   GOSUB 14000
20030   PRINT "VERY GOOD, ";NA$;"!"
20040 L = 12
20050   GOSUB 14000
20060 DE = 1500
20070   GOSUB 15000
20080 L = 24
20090   GOSUB 14000
20100   RETURN
```

```
******************************
*                            *
*            LINEAR          *
*                            *
*   -->TABLE OF VARIABLES<--  *
*                            *
******************************
```

A$ - CORRECT ANSWER
3090 4080 6080 7080 9110 10080 11080 18020 19020

B$ - MESSAGE TO SCROLL
16140 16160 16200 16230 19020 19040

BL - LENGTH OF MESSAGE
16200 16220

DE - DELAY VALUE
1060 15010 20060

HT - 'HIT' MARKER
3110 4100 6100 7100 9130 10100 11100 18010 18020 18030
18040

I - COUNTER
14010 14030 15010 15020 16040 16080 16220 16230 16250

J - COUNTER
16240 16240

K - COUNTER
19010 19060

L - LINES OF SCROLLING
1010 1040 1100 1210 2010 2090 3010 3060 4010 4050 5010
5080 6010 6050 7010 7050 8010 8110 9010 9080 10010 10050
11010 11050 12010 12040 14010 20010 20040 20080

NA$ - NAME
1090 1120 12030 20030

SA$ - STUDENT ANSWER
17040 18020

END OF VAR. LIST

(continued)

```
?
]RUN
```

                    THE METRIC SYSTEM

WHAT IS YOUR NAME?
?JOYCE

I AM HAPPY TO MEET YOU, JOYCE.

IN THIS LESSON WE WILL BE STUDYING
THE METRIC SYSTEM.

WE WILL LOOK AT THE BASIC UNITS OF
MEASUREMENT FOR LENGTH, VOLUME, AND
MASS.

PRESS ANY KEY TO CONTINUE

LET'S BEGIN WITH THE TERM 'METRIC.'

THE 'METRIC' SYSTEM GETS ITS NAME
FROM ITS BASIC UNIT OF LENGTH, THE
METER.

PRESS ANY KEY TO CONTINUE

THE METRIC SYSTEM WAS NAMED AFTER ITS
BASIC UNIT OF LENGTH, WHICH IS
THE .....

TYPE IN THE ANSWER HERE, THEN PRESS
THE RETURN KEY.
?METER

VERY GOOD, JOYCE!

THE METER IS THE METRIC SYSTEM'S
BASIC UNIT OF ....

TYPE IN THE ANSWER HERE, THEN PRESS
THE RETURN KEY.
?MASS
THE CORRECT ANSWER IS   LENGTH .

THE CORRECT ANSWER IS   LENGTH .

THE CORRECT ANSWER IS   LENGTH .

THE METER IS THE METRIC SYSTEM'S
BASIC UNIT OF ....

TYPE IN THE ANSWER HERE, THEN PRESS
THE RETURN KEY.
?LENGTH

VERY GOOD, JOYCE!

                              (continued)

THE BASIC UNIT OF VOLUME IN THE METRIC
SYSTEM IS THE 'LITER.'

THE LITER IS USED TO MEASURE LIQUIDS
AND GASES.

PRESS ANY KEY TO CONTINUE

THE BASIC UNIT FOR MEASURING VOLUMES
IN THE METRIC SYSTEM IS THE ......

TYPE IN THE ANSWER HERE, THEN PRESS
THE RETURN KEY.
?LITER

VERY GOOD, JOYCE!

THE LITER IS USUALLY USED TO MEASURE
GASES AND ....

TYPE IN THE ANSWER HERE, THEN PRESS
THE RETURN KEY.
?LIQUIDS

VERY GOOD, JOYCE!

IN THE METRIC SYSTEM, THE MEASUREMENT
OF WEIGHT IS BASED ON MASS, THE AMOUNT
OF MATTER AN OBJECT CONTAINS.

THE METRIC UNIT OF MASS IS THE 'GRAM.'

THE GRAM IS USUALLY USED TO MEASURE
SOLID THINGS.

PRESS ANY KEY TO CONTINUE

THE METRIC SYSTEM BASES THE MEASUREMENT
OF WEIGHT ON THE AMOUNT OF MATTER
AN OBJECT CONTAINS.

THIS IS CALLED .....

TYPE IN THE ANSWER HERE, THEN PRESS
THE RETURN KEY.
?WEIGHT
THE CORRECT ANSWER IS MASS .

THE CORRECT ANSWER IS   MASS .

THE CORRECT ANSWER IS   MASS .

THE METRIC SYSTEM BASES THE MEASUREMENT
OF WEIGHT ON THE AMOUNT OF MATTER
AN OBJECT CONTAINS.

THIS IS CALLED .....

(continued)

```
TYPE IN THE ANSWER HERE, THEN PRESS
THE RETURN KEY.
?MASS

VERY GOOD, JOYCE!

THE METRIC UNIT FOR MEASURING MASS
IS CALLED THE .....

TYPE IN THE ANSWER HERE, THEN PRESS
THE RETURN KEY.
?GRAM

VERY GOOD, JOYCE!


THE GRAM IS USUALLY USED TO MEASURE
THINGS WHICH ARE ......

TYPE IN THE ANSWER HERE, THEN PRESS
THE RETURN KEY.
?SOLID

VERY GOOD, JOYCE!


WE ARE FINISHED, JOYCE!
```

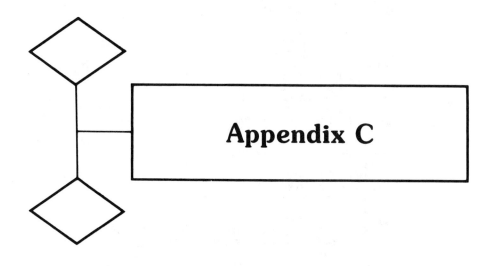

Appendix C

```
******************************
*                            *
*          BRANCHING         *
*                            *
*            ORWIG           *
******************************


10   REM   SAMPLE BRANCHING PROGRAM BY GARY ORWIG
20   REM   THIS IS A BIT SIMPLISTIC
30   REM   BUT IT SHOULD GIVE YOU THE IDEA
1000   REM   INTRODUCTION
1010 L = 24
1020   GOSUB 14000
1030   PRINT "          SYNONYMS AND ANTONYMS"
1040 L = 12
1050   GOSUB 14000
1060 DE = 2000
1070   GOSUB 15000
1080   PRINT "WHAT IS YOUR NAME?"
1090   INPUT NA$
1100 L = 24
1110   GOSUB 14000
1120   PRINT "I AM HAPPY TO MEET YOU, ";NA$;"."
1130   PRINT
1140   PRINT "WE ARE GOING TO STUDY"
1150   PRINT "SYNONYMS AND ANTONYMS IN THIS UNIT."
1160   PRINT
1170   PRINT
```

(continued)

```
1180   PRINT "BEFORE WE START, HOWEVER, I WANT"
1190   PRINT "TO CHECK TO SEE IF YOU ALREADY KNOW"
1200   PRINT "SOME THINGS ABOUT SYNONYMS AND"
1210   PRINT "ANTONYMS."
1220 L = 8
1230   GOSUB 14000
1240   GOSUB 16000
2000   REM   PRETEST
2010 L = 24
2020   GOSUB 14000
2030   PRINT "WHICH OF THE FOLLWING WORDS IS A"
2040   PRINT "SYNONYM FOR 'SLY'?"
2050   PRINT
2060   PRINT "     HEAVY"
2070   PRINT "     PRETTY"
2080   PRINT "     CUNNING"
2090   PRINT "     GENTLE"
2100 L = 12
2110   GOSUB 14000
2120   GOSUB 17000
2130   IF SA$ = "CUNNING" THEN SS = SS + 1
2140 L = 24
2150   GOSUB 14000
2160   PRINT "WHICH OF THE FOLLWING WORDS IS A"
2170   PRINT "SYNONYM FOR 'QUICK'?"
2180   PRINT
2190   PRINT "     SLOW"
2200   PRINT "     CRUEL"
2210   PRINT "     FAST"
2220   PRINT "     GENTLE"
2230 L = 12
2240   GOSUB 14000
2250   GOSUB 17000
2260   IF SA$ = "FAST" THEN SS = SS + 1
2270 L = 24
2280   GOSUB 14000
2290   PRINT "WHICH OF THE FOLLWING WORDS IS AN"
2300   PRINT "ANTONYM FOR 'SHARP'?"
2310   PRINT
2320   PRINT "     DULL"
2330   PRINT "     HOT"
2340   PRINT "     AWFUL"
2350   PRINT "     FAST"
2360 L = 12
2370   GOSUB 14000
2380   GOSUB 17000
2390   IF SA$ = "DULL" THEN AS = AS + 1
2400 L = 24
2410   GOSUB 14000
2420   PRINT "WHICH OF THE FOLLWING WORDS IS AN"
2430   PRINT "ANTONYM FOR 'HEAVY'?"
2440   PRINT
2450   PRINT "     NEAR"
2460   PRINT "     COMMON"
2470   PRINT "     LIGHT"
2480   PRINT "     LATE"
2490 L = 12
2500   GOSUB 14000
2510   GOSUB 17000
2520   IF SA$ = "LIGHT" THEN AS = AS + 1
2530   IF SS < > 2 THEN 3000
2540   IF AS < > 2 THEN 5000
```

(continued)

```
2550 L = 24
2560   GOSUB 14000
2570   PRINT "I THINK YOU KNOW THIS STUFF, "
2580   PRINT NA$;"!   I DON'T THINK YOU NEED"
2590   PRINT "TO STUDY IT ANY FURTHER."
2600   PRINT
2610   PRINT "BYE FOR NOW!"
2620 L = 12
2630   GOSUB 14000
2640   END
3000   REM   SYNONYMS
3010 L = 24
3020   GOSUB 14000
3030   PRINT "LET'S START WORKING ON SYNONYMS."
3040   PRINT
3050   PRINT "WORDS ARE SYNONYMS WHEN THEY HAVE THE"
3060   PRINT "SAME (OR ALMOST THE SAME) MEANINGS."
3070   PRINT
3080   PRINT "FOR EXAMPLE, SMART AND CLEVER"
3090   PRINT "ARE SYNONYMS."
3100 L = 14
3110   GOSUB 14000
3120   GOSUB 16000
3130 L = 24
3140   GOSUB 14000
3150   PRINT "WHY DON'T YOU TRY ONE NOW."
3160   PRINT
3170   PRINT "WHICH OF THE FOLLOWING WORDS IS"
3180   PRINT "A SYNONYM FOR THE WORD 'PRETTY?'"
3190   PRINT
3200   PRINT "      UGLY"
3210   PRINT "      CUTE"
3220   PRINT "      NEAR"
3230   PRINT "      FAR"
3240 L = 12
3250   GOSUB 14000
3260   GOSUB 17000
3270 A$ = "CUTE"
3280   GOSUB 18000
3290   IF SA$ = "UGLY" THEN   GOSUB 4000
3300   IF HT = 0 THEN   GOSUB 4500
3310   IF HT = 0 THEN 3130
3320   REM   CORRECT
3330   GOTO 5000
4000   REM   WRONG ANSWERS
4010   REM   OPPOSITE
4020 L = 24
4030   GOSUB 14000
4040   PRINT SA$;" MEANS THE OPPOSITE OF PRETTY."
4050   PRINT "WE WILL WORK WITH OPPOSITES A LITTLE"
4060   PRINT "BIT LATER."
4070   PRINT
4080   PRINT "WE WANT A WORD WHICH MEANS ALMOST"
4090   PRINT "THE SAME THING AS PRETTY."
4100   PRINT
4110 L = 12
4120   GOSUB 14000
4130   GOSUB 16000
4140   RETURN
4500   REM   WRONG ANSWER
4510 L = 24
4520   GOSUB 14000
```

(continued)

```
4530   PRINT "REMEMBER, NOW YOU WANT TO FIND A"
4540   PRINT "SYNONYM FOR THE WORD 'PRETTY.'"
4550   PRINT
4560   PRINT
4570   PRINT "SYNONYMS ARE WORDS WHICH HAVE ALMOST"
4580   PRINT "THE SAME MEANING."
4590 L = 14
4600   GOSUB 14000
4610   GOSUB 16000
4620   RETURN
5000   REM  ANTONYMS
5010   IF AS = 2 THEN 7000
5020 L = 24
5030   GOSUB 14000
5040   PRINT "LET'S WORK ON ANTONYMS NOW."
5050   PRINT
5060   PRINT "WORDS ARE ANTONYMS WHEN THEY HAVE THE"
5070   PRINT "OPPOSITE (OR ALMOST THE"
5080   PRINT "OPPOSITE) MEANINGS."
5090   PRINT
5100   PRINT "FOR EXAMPLE, BIG AND LITTLE"
5110   PRINT "ARE ANTONYMS."
5120 L = 14
5130   GOSUB 14000
5140   GOSUB 16000
5150 L = 24
5160   GOSUB 14000
5170   PRINT "WHY DON'T YOU TRY ONE NOW."
5180   PRINT
5190   PRINT "WHICH OF THE FOLLOWING WORDS IS"
5200   PRINT "AN ANTONYM FOR THE WORD 'SLENDER?'"
5210   PRINT
5220   PRINT "      THIN"
5230   PRINT "      FAST"
5240   PRINT "      FAT"
5250   PRINT "      SLOW"
5260 L = 12
5270   GOSUB 14000
5280   GOSUB 17000
5290 A$ = "FAT"
5300   GOSUB 18000
5310   IF SA$ = "THIN" THEN  GOSUB 6000
5320   IF HT = 0 THEN   GOSUB 6500
5330   IF HT = 0 THEN 5150
5340   REM  CORRECT
5350   GOTO 7000
6000   REM  WRONG ANSWERS
6010   REM  SYNONYM
6020 L = 24
6030   GOSUB 14000
6040   PRINT SA$;" MEANS THE SAME AS SLENDER."
6050   PRINT "YOU MUST STILL BE THINKING OF"
6055   PRINT "SYNONYMS!"
6070   PRINT
6080   PRINT "WE WANT A WORD WHICH MEANS ALMOST"
6090   PRINT "THE OPPOSITE OF SLENDER."
6100   PRINT
6110 L = 12
6120   GOSUB 14000
6130   GOSUB 16000
6140   RETURN
6500   REM  WRONG ANSWER
```

(continued)

```
6510 L = 24
6520  GOSUB 14000
6530  PRINT "REMEMBER, NOW YOU WANT TO FIND AN"
6540  PRINT "ANTONYM FOR THE WORD 'SLENDER.'"
6550  PRINT
6560  PRINT
6570  PRINT "ANTONYMS ARE WORDS WHICH HAVE ALMOST"
6580  PRINT "THE OPPOSITE MEANING."
6590 L = 14
6600  GOSUB 14000
6610  GOSUB 16000
6620  RETURN
7000  REM  FINISHED
7010 L = 24
7020  GOSUB 14000
7030  PRINT "WE ARE FINISHED!
7040  PRINT
7050  PRINT "I HOPE YOU HAD FUN, ";NA$;"."
7060  END
13000  REM   START OF SUBROUTINES
14000  REM    SCROLLING
14010  FOR I = 1 TO L
14020  PRINT
14030  NEXT I
14040  RETURN
15000  REM   DELAY
15010  FOR I = 1 TO DE
15020  NEXT I
15030  RETURN
16000  REM  KEY PROMPT
16010  REM  CHECK WITH NO SCROLLING
16020  VTAB 23
16030  PRINT "PRESS ANY KEY TO CONTINUE"
16040  FOR I = 1 TO 900
16050  IF  PEEK (49152) <  = 128 THEN 16080
16060  POKE 49168,0
16070  RETURN
16080  NEXT I
16090  REM  CHECK WITH SCROLLING
16100  IF  PEEK (49152) <  = 128 THEN 16130
16110  POKE 49168,0
16120  RETURN
16130  REM    ASSIGN MESSAGE TO B$
16140 B$ = "PRESS ANY KEY TO CONTINUE"
16150  GOSUB 16190
16160 B$ = "                           "
16170  GOSUB 16190
16180  GOTO 16090
16190  REM  SCROLLING ROUTINE
16200 BL =  LEN (B$)
16210  VTAB 23
16220  FOR I = 1 TO BL
16230  PRINT  MID$ (B$,I,1);
16240  FOR J = 1 TO 20: NEXT J
16250  NEXT I
16260  PRINT
16270  RETURN
17000  REM  GET STUDENT ANSWER
17010  VTAB 20
17020  PRINT "TYPE IN THE ANSWER HERE, THEN PRESS"
17030  PRINT "THE RETURN KEY."
17040  INPUT SA$
```

(continued)

```
17050   RETURN
18000   REM   JUDGE ANSWER
18010  HT = 0
18020    IF SA$ = A$ THEN HT = 1
18030    IF HT = 0 THEN   GOSUB 19000
18040    IF HT = 1 THEN   GOSUB 20000
18050   RETURN
19000   REM   WRONG ANSWER
19010    FOR K = 1 TO 3
19020  B$ = "THE CORRECT ANSWER IS   " + A$ + " ."
19030    GOSUB 16190
19040  B$ = "                                        "
19050    GOSUB 16190
19060    NEXT K
19070   RETURN
20000   REM   CORRECT ANSWER
20010  L = 24
20020    GOSUB 14000
20030    PRINT "VERY GOOD, ";NA$;"!"
20040  L = 12
20050    GOSUB 14000
20060  DE = 1500
20070    GOSUB 15000
20080  L = 24
20090    GOSUB 14000
20100    RETURN
```

```
******************************
*                            *
*         BRANCHING          *
*                            *
*    -->TABLE OF VARIABLES<-- *
*                            *
******************************
```

A$ - CORRECT ANSWER
3270 5290 18020 19020

AS - ANTONYM SCORE
2390 2390 2520 2520 2540 5010

B$ - MESSAGE FOR SCROLLING
16140 16160 16200 16230 19020 19040

BL - LENGTH OF MESSAGE
16200 16220

DE - DELAY VALUE
1060 15010 20060

HT - 'HIT' MARKER
3300 3310 5320 5330 18010 18020 18030 18040

I - COUNTER
14010 14030 15010 15020 16040 16080 16220 16230 16250

J - COUNTER
16240 16240

(continued)

```
K - COUNTER
19010 19060

L - LINES OF SCROLLING
1010 1040 1100 1220 2010 2100 2140 2230 2270 2360 2400
2490 2550 2620 3010 3100 3130 3240 4020 4110 4510 4590
5020 5120 5150 5260 6020 6110 6510 6590 7010 14010 20010
20040 20080

NA$ - NAME
1090 1120 2580 7050 20030

SA$ - STUDENT ANSWER
2130 2260 2390 2520 3290 4040 5310 6040 17040 18020

SS - SYNONYM SCORE
2130 2130 2260 2260 2530

END OF VAR. LIST
JRUN

          SYNONYMS AND ANTONYMS

WHAT IS YOUR NAME?
?JENNIFER

I AM HAPPY TO MEET YOU, JENNIFER.

WE ARE GOING TO STUDY
SYNONYMS AND ANTONYMS IN THIS UNIT.


BEFORE WE START, HOWEVER, I WANT
TO CHECK TO SEE IF YOU ALREADY KNOW
SOME THINGS ABOUT SYNONYMS AND
ANTONYMS.

PRESS ANY KEY TO CONTINUE

WHICH OF THE FOLLWING WORDS IS A
SYNONYM FOR 'SLY'?

        HEAVY
        PRETTY
        CUNNING
        GENTLE

TYPE IN THE ANSWER HERE, THEN PRESS
THE RETURN KEY.
?CUNNING

WHICH OF THE FOLLWING WORDS IS A
SYNONYM FOR 'QUICK'?

        SLOW
        CRUEL
        FAST
        GENTLE

TYPE IN THE ANSWER HERE, THEN PRESS
THE RETURN KEY.
?FAST
```

(continued)

WHICH OF THE FOLLWING WORDS IS AN
ANTONYM FOR 'SHARP'?

        DULL
        HOT
        AWFUL
        FAST

TYPE IN THE ANSWER HERE, THEN PRESS
THE RETURN KEY.
?FAST

WHICH OF THE FOLLWING WORDS IS AN
ANTONYM FOR 'HEAVY'?

        NEAR
        COMMON
        LIGHT
        LATE

TYPE IN THE ANSWER HERE, THEN PRESS
THE RETURN KEY.
?LATE

LET'S WORK ON ANTONYMS NOW.

WORDS ARE ANTONYMS WHEN THEY HAVE THE
OPPOSITE (OR ALMOST THE
OPPOSITE) MEANINGS.

FOR EXAMPLE, BIG AND LITTLE
ARE ANTONYMS.

PRESS ANY KEY TO CONTINUE

WHY DON'T YOU TRY ONE NOW.

WHICH OF THE FOLLOWING WORDS IS
AN ANTONYM FOR THE WORD 'SLENDER?'

        THIN
        FAST
        FAT
        SLOW

TYPE IN THE ANSWER HERE, THEN PRESS
THE RETURN KEY.
?THIN
THE CORRECT ANSWER IS   FAT .

THE CORRECT ANSWER IS   FAT .

THE CORRECT ANSWER IS   FAT .

THIN MEANS THE SAME AS SLENDER.
YOU MUST STILL BE THINKING OF
SYNONYMS!

WE WANT A WORD WHICH MEANS ALMOST
THE OPPOSITE OF SLENDER.

(continued)

PRESS ANY KEY TO CONTINUE

REMEMBER, NOW YOU WANT TO FIND AN
ANTONYM FOR THE WORD 'SLENDER.'

ANTONYMS ARE WORDS WHICH HAVE ALMOST
THE OPPOSITE MEANING.

PRESS ANY KEY TO CONTINUE

WHY DON'T YOU TRY ONE NOW.

WHICH OF THE FOLLOWING WORDS IS
AN ANTONYM FOR THE WORD 'SLENDER?'

        THIN
        FAST
        FAT
        SLOW

TYPE IN THE ANSWER HERE, THEN PRESS
THE RETURN KEY.
?FAT

VERY GOOD, JENNIFER!

WE ARE FINISHED!

I HOPE YOU HAD FUN, JENNIFER.

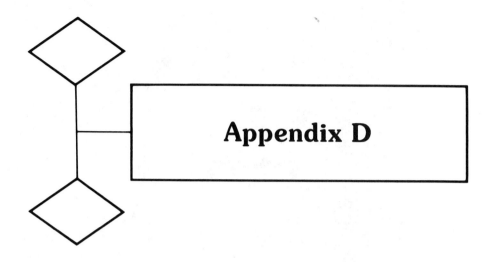

Appendix D

```
*****************************
*                           *
*        SIMULATION         *
*                           *
*          ORWIG            *
*****************************
```

```
10   REM   BALLISTIC SIMULATION BY GARY ORWIG
1000   REM   INTRODUCTION
1010 L = 2
1020   GOSUB 12000
1030   PRINT "THIS IS A PROGRAM WHICH SIMULATES THE"
1040   PRINT "FLIGHT OF A CANNON BALL."
1050   PRINT
1060   PRINT "YOU MUST SUPPLY THE ANGLE AT WHICH"
1070   PRINT "THE GUN IS TO BE FIRED.   THIS IS AN"
1080   PRINT "ANGLE EXPRESSED IN A RANGE OF "
1090   PRINT "0 TO 90 DEGREES."
1100   PRINT
1110   PRINT "IN ADDITION, YOU WILL HAVE TO DECIDE"
1120   PRINT "ON THE VELOCITY OF THE CANNON BALL."
1130   PRINT "SINCE YOU CAN VARY THE AMOUNT OF "
1140   PRINT "GUNPOWDER IN THE CANNON, THIS IS NOT"
1150   PRINT "A PROBLEM.   USUALLY VELOCITIES IN THE"
1160   PRINT "RANGE OF 200 TO 300 METERS PER SECOND"
1170   PRINT "ARE EFFECTIVE."
1180   PRINT
1190   PRINT "TO KEEP THINGS SIMPLE, WE WILL IGNORE"
```

(continued)

```
1200   PRINT "AIR FRICTION FOR NOW."
1210   PRINT
1220   PRINT "PRESS 'RETURN' OR 'ENTER'": REM  FOR PET PRESS ANY LE
       TTER BEFORE PRESSING RETURN
1230   INPUT S$
1240 L = 13
1250   GOSUB 12000
1260   PRINT "        HERE WE GO!"
1270   GOSUB 12000
1280 DE = 1000
1290   GOSUB 13000
1300 L = 24
2000   REM   MAIN PROGRAM
2010   REM   SCROLL
2020   GOSUB 11000
2030   REM   SET RANGE
2040   GOSUB 12000
2050   REM   INPUT PARAMETERS
2060   GOSUB 3000
2070   REM   CALCULATE
2080   GOSUB 4000
2090   REM   REPORT
2100   GOSUB 5000
2110   REM   PLOT
2120   GOSUB 6000
2130   REM   JUDGE RESULTS
2140   GOSUB 7000
2150   REM   HIT
2160   IF HT = 2 THEN 8000
2170   REM   CLOSE, BUT MISS
2180   IF HT = 1 THEN   GOSUB 9000
2190   REM   MISS
2200   IF HT = 0 THEN   GOSUB 10000
2210   REM   MISSED, SO TRY AGAIN
2220   GOTO 2060
3000   REM   INPUT PARAMETERS
3010   PRINT "TARGET RANGE IS ";RX;" METERS."
3020   PRINT "ENTER ELEVATION ANGLE IN DEGREES:";
3030   INPUT ED
3040   IF ED < 90 THEN 3070
3050   PRINT "YOU'RE SHOOTING THE WRONG WAY, ";NA$;"!"
3060   GOTO 3020
3070   PRINT "ENTER VELOCITY IN M/S:";
3080   INPUT VI
3090   RETURN
4000   REM   CALULATIONS
4010   REM   G IS ACCEL OF GRAVITY
4020 G = 9.80
4030   REM   CHANGE DEGREES TO RADIANS
4040 ER = ED * .0174533
4050   REM   CALC MAX HEIGHT
4060 H = (VI *  SIN (ER)) ^ 2 / (2 * G)
4070 H =  INT (H)
4080   REM   CALC TIME OF FLIGHT
4090 T = (2 * VI *  SIN (ER)) / G
4100   REM   CALC DISTANCE
4110 D =  COS (ER) * VI * T
4120 T =  INT (T)
4130 D =  INT (D)
4140   REM   REDUCE DISTANCE TO SCALE
4150 DB =  INT ((D / 200) + .5)
4160   RETURN
```

(continued)

```
5000    REM   REPORT RESULTS
5010    GOSUB 12000
5020    PRINT "                    BOOM!"
5030    GOSUB 12000
5040    PRINT
5050    PRINT "ELEVATION:          ";ED;" DEGREES"
5060    PRINT
5070    PRINT "INIT. VELOCITY:     ";VI;" M/S"
5080    PRINT
5090    PRINT "TOTAL DISTANCE:     ";D;" METERS"
5100    PRINT
5110    PRINT "MAXIMUM HEIGHT:     ";H;" METERS"
5120    PRINT
5130    PRINT "TOTAL TIME IN AIR:  ";T;" SEC."
5140    PRINT
5150    PRINT
5160    RETURN
6000    REM   PLOT RESULTS
6010    PRINT
6020    PRINT
6030    IF DB < 41 THEN 6070
6040    PRINT "             OUT OF SIGHT!"
6050    PRINT "                              >>>"
6060    GOTO 6150
6070    FOR I = 1 TO DB - 3
6080    PRINT " ";
6090    NEXT I
6100    PRINT "CRASH"
6110    FOR I = 1 TO DB - 1
6120    PRINT " ";
6130    NEXT I
6140    PRINT "#"
6150    PRINT "X%";
6160    FOR I = 1 TO DT - 4
6170    PRINT " ";
6180    NEXT I
6190    PRINT "^^^"
6200    FOR I = 1 TO 39
6210    PRINT "*";
6220    NEXT I
6230    PRINT
6240    FOR I = 1 TO DT - 1
6250    PRINT " ";
6260    NEXT I
6270    PRINT "^"
6280    FOR I = 1 TO DT - 3
6290    PRINT " ";
6300    NEXT I
6310    PRINT RX
6320    RETURN
7000    REM   JUDGE RESULTS
7010 HT = 0
7020    REM   DIRECT HIT
7030    IF DB = DT THEN HT = 2
7040    REM   NEAR MISS
7050    IF DB = DT + 1 THEN HT = 1
7060    IF DB = DT - 1 THEN HT = 1
7070    RETURN
8000    REM   REWARD
8010    FOR I = 1 TO 60
8020    PRINT "     KAPOW!!     ";
8030    NEXT I
```

(continued)

```
8040   PRINT
8050   PRINT
8060   PRINT "DIRECT HIT!"
8070  DE = 1000
8080   GOSUB 13000
8090  L = 24
8100   GOSUB 12000
8110   GOTO 14000
9000   REM   CLOSE HIT
9010   PRINT "OUCH!! DAMAGED, BUT NOT OUT!"
9020   RETURN
10000   REM   MISS
10010   PRINT "HA HA!   MISSED ME!!"
10020   RETURN
11000   REM   RANDOMIZATION OF RANGE
11010  R =   INT ( RND (1) * 11)
11020  RX = 5000 + (200 * R)
11030   REM   SET RANGE TO SCALE
11040  DT =   INT ((RX / 200) + .5)
11050   RETURN
12000   REM   SCROLLING
12010   FOR I = 1 TO L
12020   PRINT
12030   NEXT I
12040   RETURN
13000   REM   DELAY
13010   FOR I = 1 TO DE
13020   NEXT I
13030   RETURN
14000   REM   CLOSING
14010   PRINT "WANT TO TRY AGAIN?"
14020   PRINT "TYPE IN 'YES' OR 'NO'"
14030   INPUT S$
14040   IF S$ = "YES" THEN 2000
14050   PRINT "BYE FOR NOW.   I HOPE YOU HAD FUN!"
```

```
******************************
*                            *
*         SIMULATION         *
*                            *
*    -->TABLE OF VARIABLES<-- *
*                            *
******************************
```

D - DISTANCE
4110 4130 4130 4150 5090

DB - DISTANCE TO SCALE
4150 6030 6070 6110 7030 7050 7060

DE - DELAY VALUE
1280 8070 13010

DT - DISTANCE TO TARGET SCALE
6160 6240 6280 7030 7050 7060 11040

ED - ELEVATION IN DEGREES
3030 3040 4040 5050

(continued)

```
ER - ELEVATION IN RADIANS
4040 4060 4090 4110

G - ACCEL. OF GRAVITY
4020 4060 4090

H - MAX. HEIGHT
4060 4070 4070 5110

HT - 'HIT' MARKER
2160 2180 2200 7010 7030 7050 7060

I - COUNTER
6070 6090 6110 6130 6160 6180 6200 6220 6240 6260 6280
6300 8010 8030 12010 12030 13010 13020

L - LINES OF SCROLLING
1010 1240 1300 8090 12010

NA$ - NAME
3050

R - RANDOM NUMBER
11010 11020

RX - RANGE
3010 6310 11020 11040

S$ - STUDENT RESPONSE
1230 14030 14040

T - TIME OF FLIGHT
4090 4110 4120 4120 5130

VI - INITIAL VELOCITY
3080 4060 4090 4110 5070

END OF VAR. LIST

]
]RUN

THIS IS A PROGRAM WHICH SIMULATES THE
FLIGHT OF A CANNON BALL.

YOU MUST SUPPLY THE ANGLE AT WHICH
THE GUN IS TO BE FIRED.   THIS IS AN
ANGLE EXPRESSED IN A RANGE OF
0 TO 90 DEGREES.

IN ADDITION, YOU WILL HAVE TO DECIDE
ON THE VELOCITY OF THE CANNON BALL.
SINCE YOU CAN VARY THE AMOUNT OF
GUNPOWDER IN THE CANNON, THIS IS NOT
A PROBLEM.   USUALLY VELOCITIES IN THE
RANGE OF 200 TO 300 METERS PER SECOND
ARE EFFECTIVE.

TO KEEP THINGS SIMPLE, WE WILL IGNORE
AIR FRICTION FOR NOW.

PRESS 'RETURN' OR 'ENTER'
```

(continued)

```
?

        HERE WE GO!


TARGET RANGE IS 5000 METERS.
ENTER ELEVATION ANGLE IN DEGREES:?40
ENTER VELOCITY IN M/S:?250


        BOOM!


ELEVATION:          40 DEGREES

INIT. VELOCITY:     250 M/S

TOTAL DISTANCE:     6280 METERS

MAXIMUM HEIGHT:     1317 METERS

TOTAL TIME IN AIR:  32 SEC.


                            CRASH
                             #
X%                              ^^^
***************************************
                         ^
                        5000
HA HA!  MISSED ME!!
TARGET RANGE IS 5000 METERS.
ENTER ELEVATION ANGLE IN DEGREES:?35
ENTER VELOCITY IN M/S:?200


        BOOM!


ELEVATION:          35 DEGREES

INIT. VELOCITY:     200 M/S

TOTAL DISTANCE:     3835 METERS

MAXIMUM HEIGHT:     671 METERS

TOTAL TIME IN AIR:  23 SEC.


            CRASH
             #
X%                      ^^^
***************************************
                     ^
                    5000
HA HA!  MISSED ME!!
TARGET RANGE IS 5000 METERS.
ENTER ELEVATION ANGLE IN DEGREES:?40
ENTER VELOCITY IN M/S:?220


        BOOM!
```

(continued)

```
ELEVATION:          40 DEGREES

INIT. VELOCITY:     220 M/S

TOTAL DISTANCE:     4863 METERS

MAXIMUM HEIGHT:     1020 METERS

TOTAL TIME IN AIR:  28 SEC.

                        CRASH
                          #
X%                       ^^^
*************************************
                         ^
                        5000
OUCH!! DAMAGED, BUT NOT OUT!
TARGET RANGE IS 5000 METERS.
ENTER ELEVATION ANGLE IN DEGREES:?40
ENTER VELOCITY IN M/S:?225

               BOOM!


ELEVATION:          40 DEGREES

INIT. VELOCITY:     225 M/S

TOTAL DISTANCE:     5087 METERS

MAXIMUM HEIGHT:     1067 METERS

TOTAL TIME IN AIR:  29 SEC.

                        CRASH
                          #
X%                       ^^^
*************************************
                         ^
                        5000
     KAPOW!!         KAPOW!!         KAPOW!!         KAPOW!!
KAPOW!!         KAPOW!!         KAPOW!!         KAPOW!!         KAPOW
!!        KAPOW!!         KAPOW!!         KAPOW!!         KAPOW!!
     KAPOW!!         KAPOW!!         KAPOW!!         KAPOW!!
          KAPOW!!         KAPOW!!         KAPOW!!         KAPO
W!!        KAPOW!!         KAPOW!!         KAPOW!!         KAPOW!!
     KAPOW!!         KAPOW!!         KAPOW!!         KAPOW!!
  KAPOW!!         KAPOW!!         KAPOW!!         KAPOW!!
          KAPOW!!         KAPOW!!         KAPOW!!         KAPOW!!
     KAPOW!!         KAPOW!!         KAPOW!!         KAPOW!!
  KAPOW!!         KAPOW!!         KAPOW!!         KAPOW!!         KAP
OW!!        KAPOW!!         KAPOW!!         KAPOW!!
          KAPOW!!         KAPOW!!         KAPOW!!         KAPOW!!
   KAPOW!!         KAPOW!!         KAPOW!!         KAPOW!!         KA
POW!!        KAPOW!!         KAPOW!!

DIRECT HIT!

WANT TO TRY AGAIN?
TYPE IN 'YES' OR 'NO'
?NO
BYE FOR NOW.  I HOPE YOU HAD FUN!
```

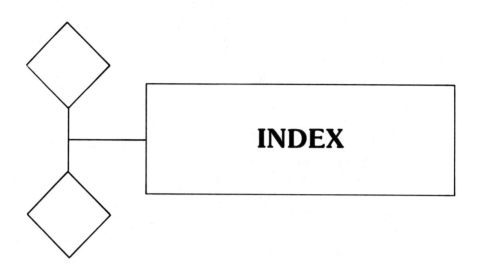

INDEX